**Grandmother Mary (Joyce) Kelly, c. 1**

# Our Joyce & O'Brien Ancestors
# Loughaconeera, County Galway

### Joyce V. Kelly, Ph.D.
### (Seoige O'Ceallaigh in Irish)

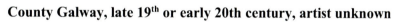

**County Galway, late 19th or early 20th century, artist unknown**

Cover photos:
Top:  Sean O'Briain (John O'Brien in English), his daughter-in-law, Annie (Nan) Sullivan (wife of Sean's son Peadar O'Briain), and granddaughters Nora and Barbara, at home in Loughaconeera, 1930. Sean was an uncle of our paternal grandmother, Mary (Joyce) Kelly, a farmer-fisherman, and a highly regarded sgéalaidhthe (traditional Gaelic storyteller). O'Briain spoke only Irish and is referred to by the Irish spelling of his surname.
Bottom:  One of many abandoned houses in Loughaconeera in 2018. Houses with turf or thatch roofs deteriorated quickly if not maintained.

Source: http://www.oidhreachtlca.ie/, the Loughaconeera Heritage Website.

This Family History includes extensive quotations, data, maps, and records—all are attributed. Images also are attributed, or they were provided by family members, or they are in the public domain. Black and white photos were colorized using a feature on MyHeritage.com.

Cover Design: Ken Falk Marketing and Communications

ISBN: 978-1-957468-26-6

# Table of Contents

# Appendices

See https://www.ancestry.com/family-tree/tree/160255584?cfpid=282094565936is **for my full Theobald/Kelly/McKelvey/Joyce family tree. My abbreviated Joyce/O'Brien family tree is on p. 13.**

# Introduction

This family history describes the discovery and documentation of the ancestors and ancestral home in Ireland of our paternal grandmother, Mary (Joyce) Kelly. My brother Jim and I recently became interested in our family history and began researching our four grandparents. We were unaware of the location of Mary's ancestral home and her ancestors in Ireland because our father did not have any records or photos of his mother, who died in 1918. We also had not asked him, before he died in 1967, about her parents, grandparents, and place of birth in Ireland. The preliminary family tree below summarizes what we knew about Mary when Jim and I began researching her history. Throughout this essay, "we" refers to my brother Jim, sisters Kate and Julie, and me, and "our" ancestors refers to ancestors of the four of us.

## Mary (Joyce) Kelly Preliminary Family Tree

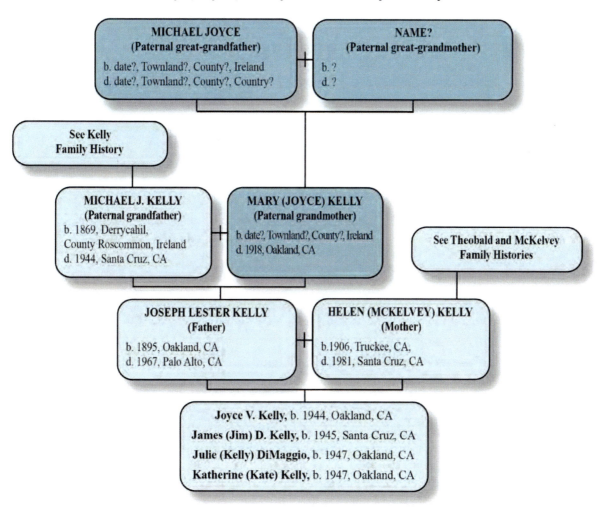

This Family History focuses on our paternal grandmother, Mary (Joyce) Kelly, and her ancestors. The three darker colored boxes in the preliminary family tree above distinguish them. After completing this research, I developed two "final" family trees for our Joyce/O'Brien ancestors-an abbreviated tree on page 13 of this document and a complete, fully-documented, tree at **https://www.ancestry.com/family-tree/tree/160255584?cfpid=282094565936is**

Our documentation of Mary (Joyce) Kelly's family history began with her arrival from Ireland in New York City in 1888 when she was nearly 16 years old. Mary was one of hundreds of thousands of young girls who left Ireland in the 19th century because agricultural villages did not offer many opportunities to marry or work outside the home. Relatives who emigrated earlier provided money for the passage, a home, and employment opportunities in America.

After arriving in New York, Mary traveled to California where she likely married our grandfather, Michael Kelly, in 1892/93, although we could not verify their marriage. During the 1900 and 1910 U.S. Federal Censuses, Mary and Michael lived in Oakland, California, and had five children including our father, Joseph. Mary died of heart disease in 1918, when she was 45 years old.

My brother Jim and sisters Kate and Julie, and I wish that we had learned more about our ancestors when our parents, aunts, and uncles were alive, but they were not comfortable discussing family history, and we were not curious. In 2018, Jim became interested and began researching our four grandparents. He invited me to join him after learning that 17th and 18th century ancestors of our maternal grandmother, Josephine (Theobald) McKelvey, had lived near my home in Maryland.

We knew that our paternal grandfather, Michael Kelly, and his ancestors were born in Derrycahill in County Roscommon, Ireland. But it took time and extensive research to identify the ancestors and locations of the ancestral homes of our paternal grandmother, Mary Joyce, and of our maternal grandparents–the Theobalds and McKelveys. That research is nearly complete. Family histories of the Kellys, Theobalds, and McKelveys are forthcoming.

Initially, Jim and I used traditional genealogical records to research Mary Joyce, but we could not identify her townland in Ireland. The research did not progress until my DNA matched with previously unknown genetic cousins who had well-documented family trees showing that their ancestor Mary Joyce originated in Loughaconeera in County Galway.

This family history integrates analyses of genealogical records and genetic genealogy[1] to present findings about our paternal grandmother and the evidence supporting those findings.[2] The first 28 pages summarize my research processes, findings, and documentation.[3] Appendices One through Four include documentation that is too extensive to include in the research summary. Appendix One lists locations of genealogical records in County Galway and includes birth, baptismal, and death records for several of Mary's brothers and sisters (our granduncles and grandaunts). Appendix Two includes excerpts from a report by a distant cousin, David G. Riley, independently verifying our genealogical findings about Mary's ancestors and cousins. Appendix Three is a

---

[1] Genetic genealogy combines genealogical DNA testing with traditional genealogical and historical records to infer relationships among individuals. Sources: The International Society of Genetic Genealogy wiki and *Guide to DNA Testing and Genetic Genealogy*, Blaine T. Bettinger, Family Tree, 2016.

[2] My full family tree is at https://www.ancestry.com/family-tree/tree/160255584?cfpid=282094565936is, with 292 family members, 408 records, and 68 images. My abbreviated Joyce/O'Brien family tree is on page 13 below.

[3] See the copyright page for sources and attributions.

family narrative by another distant cousin, Joseph Halloran, describing the lives of Mary's aunts, uncles, sisters, nieces, and nephews in Chicago.

Appendix Four presents the DNA Proof Argument supporting the Loughaconeera, County Galway origin of our paternal grandmother, Mary Joyce. Throughout this research, I employed the Genealogical Proof Standard (GPS)–the gold standard for developing credible, valid family histories. Components of the GPS are "reasonably exhaustive research; complete and accurate source citations; analysis and correlation of all relevant evidence, emphasizing primary sources; resolution of conflicting evidence; and soundly reasoned, coherently written conclusions."[4]

Historical narratives add meat to the bones of family trees and records. But our ancestors were illiterate and poor and did not leave letters or other records and others did not write about them. Sean O'Brien, Mary Joyce's uncle (our 2x great uncle) and a highly regarded *sgéalaidhthe* (traditional Gaelic storyteller), is an exception. Appendices Five and Six contain three of Sean O'Briain's folktales, collected and transcribed by a folklorist (Appendix Five) and by one of his granddaughters (Appendix Six). Appendix Seven is a historical narrative describing the lives of farmer-fishermen, like our ancestors. Appendix Eight chronicles the Lynches of Barna House, the landowners of Loughaconeera; and Appendix Nine summarizes Galway City's early history.

**Joyce V, Kelly, Ph.D., October 2021, Silver Spring, Maryland**

**My brother, sisters and me—Jim, Kate, Joyce, and Julie (Kelly) DiMaggio, 2006**

**Throughout this essay, "our" refers to ancestors of the four of us.**

---

[4] *Genealogy Standards, Second Edition*, Board for Certification of Genealogists, Ancestry.com, NY 2019.

# Joyce & O'Brien Ancestors

This essay provides the history of our paternal grandmother, Mary (Joyce) Kelly, her ancestors, and County Galway where they lived. My brother Jim and I collected records for Mary from the time she arrived in America, but we could not identify her origins in Ireland until DNA matching led me to Peggy Calhoun, who shared with me her Joyce line in Loughaconeera. See page 13 for an abbreviated Joyce/O'Brien family tree. My complete Theobald/Kelly/McKelvey/Joyce tree is at: https://www.ancestry.com/family-tree/tree/160255584?cfpid=282094565936is.

## Sources for the Lineage of Mary Joyce's Ancestors

Mary immigrated to America in 1888 when she was nearly 16 years old, having been born in 1872, according to her birth record. Her death certificate shows that she was born in 1871 and died on 28 July 1918 at "about 47" in Oakland, California. Her husband Michael Kelly, her father Michael Joyce, and her unnamed mother were born in Ireland.

**Mary (Joyce) Kelly's death certificate, obtained in 1994 by our sister Julie from the State of California**

Jim, our sisters Julie and Kate, and I located five records for Mary (Joyce) Kelly in the United States–her 1918 death and burial certificates, 1900 and 1910 U.S. Census entries, and 1888 immigration record. Mary was buried on 30 July 1918 at St. Mary's Cemetery, located at 4529 Howe Street in Oakland. After obtaining Mary's death certificate in 1994, our sister Julie visited the cemetery and copied the record of the Kelly family burial plot, located in Section R, Row 4.

**St. Mary's Cemetery record of the Kelly family burial plot**

The table below is my transcription of the cemetery's record.[5] I added the relationship of each person to our father based on family and Ancestry.com records, with question marks when relationships are not definitive. Note that two ancestors died in their 20s, three died in their 30s, and one died in her 40s. In 1900, U.S. life expectancy was only 47 years, primarily reflecting medical treatment for heart disease, tuberculosis, the flu, and other health problems at that time.

**My transcription of the cemetery's record**

| Name | Birth place | Age | Burial date | Plot | Relation to our father |
|------|-------------|-----|-------------|------|------------------------|
| Mary McCarthy | Ireland | 32 | 25 Nov 1903 | 78 | aunt? |
| Mary Kelly | Ireland | abt 47 | 30 July 1918 | 19 | mother |
| Hazel I. Kelly | ? | 21 | 21 Nov 1928 | 79 | sister-in-law? |
| Ethel Pinnella | Calif | 22 | 9 Mar 1927 | 18 | sister |
| Harry Kelly | Calif | 38 | 15 June 1929 | 78 | brother |
| Ida Kelly | ? | 34 | 6 Sept 1935 | 74 | first wife |
| Michael Kelly | Ireland | 76 | 12 Aug 1944 | 19 | father |

---

[5] Mary's reported birthdate on the 1900 U.S. Federal Census was 1873, making her 45 years old at death. Until relatively recently, reported birth dates and ages differed because many people were unsure of their birth dates.

**Mary's Birth, Immigration, and Marriage Dates on the 1900 U.S. Federal Census**[6]

Michael Joseph and Mary (Joyce) Kelly rented a house at 836 Brush Street, Oakland, California (address not shown below) in 1900, with our father, Joseph age four, his two brothers, and Michael's brother James who emigrated from Ireland six years earlier, in 1893 (two final columns). Mary reported her birth date as October 1873 and her age as 26. They reported being married for seven years, indicating that they married in 1892/93. A marriage date of 1892/93 is consistent with the 1894 birth of their first child, Arthur. Mary reported having three children in 1900 (middle column), all of whom were living. She emigrated from Ireland in 1888, 11 years before the 1900 Census (final column). The 1890 U.S. Federal census likely had useful information, but most of it was destroyed in a fire.

**1900 U.S Federal census record for Michael Kelly's family, from Ancestry.com**

| | | | | | | | | | | | | | | | | |
|---|---|---|---|---|---|---|---|---|---|---|---|---|---|---|---|---|
| Kelley, Michael J | Head | W | M | Aug | 1871 | 28 | M | 7 | | | Ireland | Ireland | Ireland | 1889 | 10 |
| —, Mary A. | Wife | W | F | Oct | 1873 | 26 | M | 7 | 3 | 3 | Ireland | Ireland | Ireland | 1888 | 11 |
| —, Arthur | Son | W | M | Sept | 1894 | 5 | S | | | | California | Ireland | Ireland | | |
| —, Joseph | Son | W | M | Feb | 1896 | 4 | S | | | | California | Ireland | Ireland | | |
| —, Harold | Son | W | M | Mar | 1899 | 1 | S | | | | California | Ireland | Ireland | | |
| —, James | Brother | W | M | July | 1875 | 24 | S | | | | Ireland | Ireland | Ireland | 1893 | 6 |

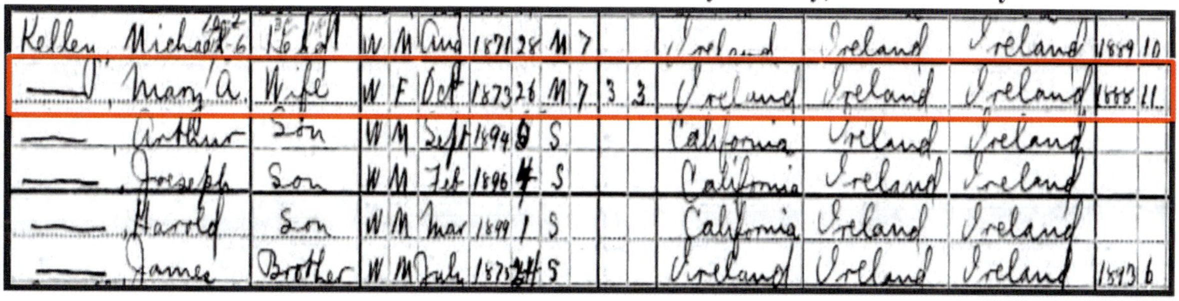

The growing Kelly family rented a house at 216 Telegraph Avenue, Oakland, California in 1910. Mary reported being the same age as her husband, 39 years old (she likely was 36 years old). They reported being married for 17 years in 1910, indicating that they married in 1892/93. Michael was the proprietor of a saloon and Mary was home with their children. Photos on the next page show the area of Oakland where the Kellys lived and worked in the late 19th and early 20th centuries.

**1910 U.S. Federal census record for Michael Kelly's family, from Ancestry.com**

| | | | | | | | | | |
|---|---|---|---|---|---|---|---|---|---|
| Kelley, Michael M | Head | M | W | 39 | M1 | 17 | | | Ire. Ireland |
| —, Mary | Wife | F | W | 39 | M1 | 17 | 5 | 5 | Ire. Irish |
| —, Arthur | Son | M | W | 16 | S | | | | California |
| —, Joseph | Son | M | W | 14 | S | | | | California |
| —, Harold | Son | M | W | 11 | S | | | | California |
| —, Jennie | Daughter | F | W | 9 | S | | | | California |
| —, Ethel | Daughter | F | W | 5 | S | | | | California |

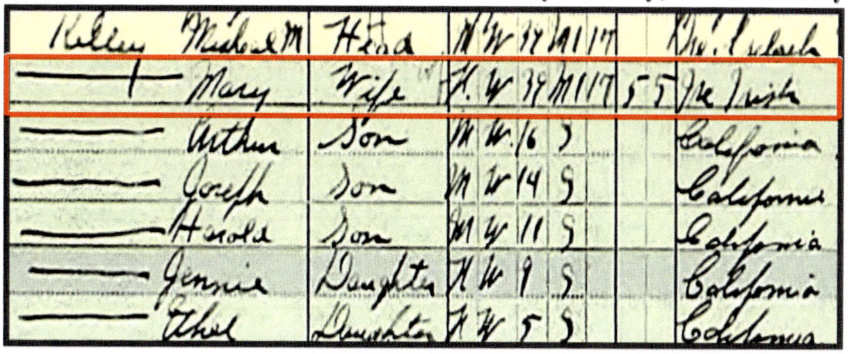

[6] Our sister Kate obtained addresses for Mary Joyce and Michael Kelly in old Oakland telephone directories. Mary lived at 1405 Webster Street between 1889/90 and 1892/93; her future husband, Michael, lived at 1355 10th Street.

**Circa 1900 photos of Oakland, near where Mary, Michael, and their children lived and worked**

**North on Telegraph Avenue**

**Hotel Albany at 15th and Broadway, looking east**     **North on Washington St. towards City Hall**

## Mary Joyce's 1888 Immigration to America

On the 1900 U.S. Federal Census, Mary reported immigrating to America in 1888.[7] At the time, she was nearly 16 years old. Our brother Jim located her immigration record (next page). Mary sailed on the *City of Rome*, from Cobh (renamed Queenstown by the British in 1849. In 1921, the Irish Free State restored the Gaelic name for Cove, the city's pre-1849 name.) Mary arrived in New York City in August 1888. We don't know why, how, or when Mary traveled from New York to Oakland, California, but we do know that her future husband, Michael Joseph Kelly, immigrated to Oakland in 1889–one year after Mary–per the 1900 U.S. Federal Census.[8] When we were children, our mother told us that Mary's and Michael's families were acquainted in Ireland.

---

[7] Nearly 4.5 million Irish arrived in America between 1820 and 1930. See https://www.loc.gov/classroom-materials/immigration/irish/irish-catholic-immigration-to-america/.

[8] Michael initially lived and worked with his uncle James who immigrated to Oakland in 1867, per U.S. Census data, the 1890 Oakland Residents' Directory, and family stories. This would have prompted Mary to settle there. In contrast, Mary's aunt Sara O'Brien emigrated to Chicago in 1882; married Thomas Keaney; and later helped Mary's three sisters and brother settle in Chicago near the Keaneys. Sarah may also have sponsored Mary and the group she traveled with–see page 5. **See Appendix 3, page 42** for a description of their lives in Chicago.

**Irish emigrants before sailing for New York from Cobh (Queenstown from 1849-1921), Co. Cork**
1874 engraving published in the *Illustrated London News*

**Transcript of Mary Joyce's 1888 immigration record (left) on the *City of Rome* (right)**

| | |
|---|---|
| Name: | Mary Joyce |
| Arrival Date: | 3 Aug 1888 |
| Birth Date: | abt 1873 |
| Age: | 15 |
| Gender: | Female |
| Ethnicity/ Nationality: | Irish |
| Place of Origin: | Ireland |
| Port of Departure: | Liverpool, England and Queenstown, Ireland |
| Destination: | USA |
| Port of Arrival: | New York, New York, USA |
| Ship Name: | City of Rome |

**Source:** "New York Passenger Lists, 1820-1891," database with images, DS/FamilySearch.org.

Jim Hollarn of the Rosmuc Area Genealogy and DNA Facebook Group reviewed a draft of this essay and he researched the passenger list. Jim observed that six passengers on the *City of Rome* registered and likely traveled together because the two youngest children would not have traveled alone. Norah and/or Eliza may have been relatives and/or escorts; Bridget Joyce may have been related to Mary; and the two "Heany" children may have been related to Thomas Keaney, Mary's uncle by marriage to her aunt, Sarah (O'Brien) Keaney, who emigrated to Chicago in 1882. If Mary was traveling with relatives of Thomas Keaney, she likely accompanied them to the Keaney's home in Chicago before departing for Oakland. But I could not verify this supposition.

**Passenger list (names, ages)–excerpt and my transcription, *City of Rome*, arr. New York, 3 Aug. 1888**

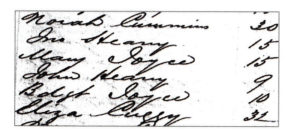

| 602 Norah Cummins | 30 |
|---|---|
| 603 J?? Heany | 15 |
| 604 Mary Joyce | 15 |
| 605 John Heany | 9 |
| 606 Bdgt Joyce | 10 |
| 607 Eliza Cully | 32 |

# Seeking the Irish Location of Mary Joyce's Ancestors with Genealogical Records

Mary's death certificate listed her father as Michael Joyce but did not identify her mother. Our sister Kate searched for the 1892/93 marriage certificate of Mary Joyce and Michael Kelly, hoping it would provide the maiden name of Mary's mother to facilitate our Irish research. Mary Joyce and Michael Kelly lived in Oakland in Alameda County, but the County has no record of their marriage. Kate also requested a search of likely Church marriage records but found none.[9] She then checked in San Francisco County–all pre-1906 County records were destroyed in the San Francisco earthquake and fires. Finally, Kate checked with the San Francisco Public Library and Catholic Archdiocese of San Francisco. None of them had a marriage record for the couple.

Much later, I extended Kate's research by hiring a genealogist at the California Genealogical Society to search other sources, including subscription newspaper websites, and records for the Chicago area, where Mary's aunt and sisters settled. The genealogist found no record of an 1892/93 marriage of Mary Joyce and Michael Kelly in California or Chicago. However, by that time, I had identified our Joyce ancestors and provided my Joyce line to the genealogist in California who located other relevant records in Ireland and Chicago that I already had collected.

Because Mary and Michael Joyce are common names in Ireland, we needed to identify Mary's townland and county of birth. Jim and I independently searched Irish records on these genealogical websites–Ancestry.com, FamilySearch.org, MyHeritage.com, RootsIreland.ie, Findmypast.com, and IrishGenealogy.ie. Using the following search terms, we identified a dozen pairs: "Mary Joyce, born 1870-1875, Ireland" and "emigrated to America in 1888" with "father Michael Joyce."

We eliminated most pairs because there were no additional records, or the daughter Mary: (1) remained in Ireland after our Mary's 1888 emigration; (2) died in Ireland; or (3) died in England or in the states of New York, Massachusetts, or Kentucky. Finally, five father-daughter pairs remained including two Mary Joyces in Galway City with a father Michael Joyce.[10] After further research, I believed that our Mary Joyce was one of these two because several of my cousins posted undocumented family trees to Ancestry showing that our grandmother Mary Joyce was born in Galway City to father Michael Joyce and mother Jane Ellwood.[11] When I could not validate this, I hired Clare Doyle of Wild Atlantic Way Genealogy in County Galway. She did locate a possible family, but their daughter Mary died young. At that point, we discontinued our research.

---

[9] Roman Catholic marriage records in Oakland and San Francisco must be obtained from individual churches. Michael and Mary may have married at one of two parish churches near their homes, but those churches closed before 2008 when the new Cathedral of Christ the Light opened nearby. Kate inquired there, but they have no record.

[10] Jim wrote the following while visiting Ireland with his wife Robin in 2019: "Mary Joyce is likely from Joyce Country in Connemara, northwest of Galway City, possibly Clifden or Oughterard. These are cities where a Mary Joyce was born in 1873 to a father named Michael Joyce." (Note from Joyce: Galway City and Annaghdown, also meet these criteria).

[11] I wasted several months following this false lead before connecting with Peggy Calhoun, of the Rosmuc Facebook Group, who shared her well-documented family tree of our Mary Joyce, described below.

# Finding the Irish Location of Mary Joyce's Ancestors with DNA Test Results

During 2020, Jim encouraged my sisters and me to take DNA tests. We tested at FamilyTreeDNA (Jim and me), AncestryDNA (Jim and me), MyHeritage (Julie and me), and 23andMe (Kate). Each company identifies DNA matches, showing degrees of relatedness to DNA-matched individuals who tested at the same company. In additions, Jim's and my Ancestry DNA tests[12] report: (1) an Ethnicity Estimate, showing broad geographic origins of a tester's ancestors over the past 500–1,000 years. My Estimate is 80% Ireland and 20% Scotland.[13] Jim's is 100% Ireland; and (2) Genetic Communities, showing specific geographic origins of a tester's more recent ancestors.

Jim's and my Ancestry Genetic Communities are identical, with ancestors originating in Galway, Lough Mask, Lough Corrib, North and South Connemara, and the South Connemara Islands in Western Galway. (See two maps on the following page.) **Later, DNA match data identified a Mary/Michael Joyce pair who resided in this area and had not appeared during our initial search of genealogical records.** Appendix Four, page 46, provides a DNA Genealogical Proof Argument[14] supporting Mary Joyce's origin in this area.

Jim's and my Genetic Communities apply to ancestors of Mary Joyce because we have verified that ancestors of our other grandparents lived in England until 1641, County Donegal until the mid-1700s, or County Roscommon until 1890. Further, 1901 Irish census data, graphed on a map by Barry Griffin below, show a high concentration of Joyce families in western County Galway.

**County Galway in Ireland (left) and proportion of residents with the surname Joyce in 1901 (right)**

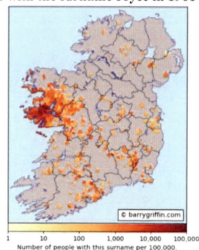

---

[12] Autosomal (atDNA) tests can be taken by men and women and include all ancestral lines because people inherit 50% of their DNA from each parent. AtDNA tests can connect to known ancestors going back to six generations.

[13] I later learned that Mary Joyce's grandmother (my 2x GG), Bridget (Davis) Joyce, was born in Scotland.

[14] A Genealogical Proof Argument uses valid data in an extensive documented narrative to support research findings. *Genealogy Standards, Second Edition*, Board for Certification of Genealogists, Ancestry.com, New York, 2019.

**My Ethnicity Estimate, and Jim's and My Genetic Communities on Ancestry.com[15]**

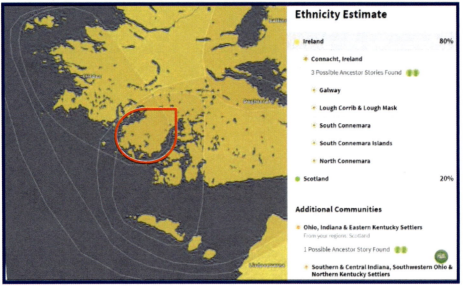

The area circled in red on the maps is a peninsula–Iorras Ainbhtheach[16]–in Connemara, the western part of County Galway. It is the center of Jim's and my Genetic Communities, defined by the intersection of five of six circles of origin (dotted white lines above). These Genetic Communities reflect Jim's and my DNA matches to Ancestry's entire DNA database, including 531,495 Ancestry DNA testers with ancestors in this area. With two sets of DNA–Jim's and mine–and a large reference group, our Genetic Communities designation is robust.

**West County Galway Ancestry Genetic Communities for Jim and me**

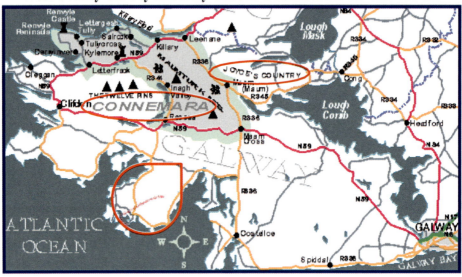

---

[15] "Additional communities" on the sidebar reflect matches with descendants of our English grandparent.

[16] Iorras Ainbhtheach is the largest peninsula in Connemara and contains the townland of **Loughaconeera.**

My FamilyTreeDNA match results show a relationship of 442 cMs[17] with a Dan Halloran who also tested at FamilyTree. When I contacted him, Dan told me that his grandfather, Patrick Halloran, was born in Rosmuc[18] in County Galway. At the time, I believed that "our" Mary Joyce originated in Galway City and I did not pursue a possible Rosmuc connection.

When Dan and I could not identify a common ancestor, I sought the help of genetic genealogist Terri Stern, founder of My Genealogy Tutor. Terri uploaded company-specific DNA test results for my brother, sisters, and me to GEDmatch,[19] resulting in dozens of new matches, including with a Joe Kelly. I emailed Joe's contact, Noel Murphy, to explore our Kelly line. Noel invited me to join the Rosmuc Area Genealogy and DNA Facebook Group that he co-founded because Joe Kelly belongs to the Group. After I joined, Noel ran the GEDmatch kits of my brother, sisters and me with the Matchmaker tool to identify additional matches with members of the Group.

Noel quickly contacted me because he thought that another Group member, Peggy Calhoun, included our Joyce line in her tree, based on my strong match with Dan Halloran, whose kit Peggy manages. After I posted our Matchmaker results to the Group, Peggy contacted me about our possible common Joyce line based on my DNA matches with members of the Rosmuc Group.[20] Later, Peggy shared her family tree (next page) and records confirming our shared Joyce line.

---

[17] Centimorgans (cMs) measure relationships between DNA matched individuals. I later confirmed that Dan and I are second cousins. On average, second cousins share about 229 cMs with a range of 41-592 cMs. Our high value of 442 cMs may reflect endogamy in western Galway villages where intermarriages occurred among extended families.

[18] Rosmuc is a peninsula, a village, and a Catholic Parish, see **Appendix One, Administrative Districts, page 30.**

[19] GEDmatch is an online service where genealogists upload company-specific autosomal DNA test results (e.g from Ancestry or FamilyTreeDNA) to search for DNA matches and other comparisons with others who also uploaded their company-specific DNA test results. GEDmatch comparisons are not limited to the same DNA testing company.

[20] Peggy is Dan Halloran's second cousin on the Halloran side. She and I do not match, but her aunt and I share 16.7cMs.

**The Joyce and O'Brien lines from Peggy Calhoun's Ancestry tree, used with permission**

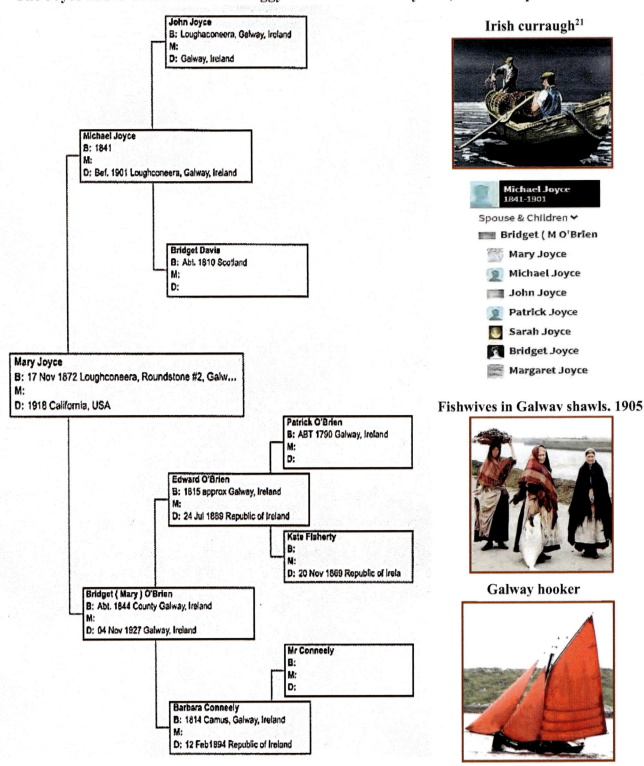

**John Joyce**
B: Loughaconeera, Galway, Ireland
M:
D: Galway, Ireland

**Michael Joyce**
B: 1841
M:
D: Bef. 1901 Loughconeera, Galway, Ireland

**Bridget Davis**
B: Abt. 1810 Scotland
M:
D:

**Mary Joyce**
B: 17 Nov 1872 Loughconeera, Roundstone #2, Galw...
M:
D: 1918 California, USA

**Patrick O'Brien**
B: ABT 1790 Galway, Ireland
M:
D:

**Edward O'Brien**
B: 1815 approx Galway, Ireland
M:
D: 24 Jul 1889 Republic of Ireland

**Kate Flaherty**
B:
M:
D: 20 Nov 1869 Republic of Irela

**Bridget ( Mary ) O'Brien**
B: Abt. 1844 County Galway, Ireland
M:
D: 04 Nov 1927 Galway, Ireland

**Mr Conneely**
B:
M:
D:

**Barbara Conneely**
B: 1814 Camus, Galway, Ireland
M:
D: 12 Feb1894 Republic of Ireland

**Irish curraugh[21]**

**Michael Joyce**
1841-1901

Spouse & Children ⌄

Bridget ( M O'Brien
Mary Joyce
Michael Joyce
John Joyce
Patrick Joyce
Sarah Joyce
Bridget Joyce
Margaret Joyce

**Fishwives in Galway shawls. 1905**

**Galway hooker**

---

[21] The curragh was the most common boat on Galway Bay until the mid-20th century. It is a keel-less rowboat, with hide (later, canvas and now, nylon) covering a wooden frame. Curraghs are small enough to be carried, so do not require a harbor, but they are not suitable for offshore fishing. When the Government installed piers, fishermen might have upgraded to larger boats, but they could not afford them.

The Joyce line on Peggy's tree shows a Mary Joyce born on 17 November 1872 in Loughaconeera (Loch Con Aortha in Irish) marked in red on both maps below. Rosduff (Ros Dubh in Irish), the home of the Hallorans and other relatives, is marked in green on both maps. The families lived on the shores of Kilkieran Bay. Photos of Galway fisherman and fishwives are on pp. 10 and 71.

**Seaside locations of Loughaconeera[22] (Joyces) and Rosduff (Hallorans and other ancestors).**
See "Rosduff, Keeloges Old, County Galway, Ireland" on Google maps.

**This map by former Connemara resident Tim Robinson shows Loch Con Aortha and Ros Dubh**

The distance between the two villages is less than four miles by sea and six miles by land.

According to Peggy's family tree on page 10, Mary's parents were Michael Joyce and Bridget Mary (O'Brien) Joyce of Loughaconeera. Mary was the oldest of seven children and the first to emigrate. Michael and Bridget's fifth child, Sarah Joyce, b. 1882, emigrated from Loughaconeera to Chicago where she married Patrick Halloran from Rossduff in Rosmuc Parish. Thus, Dan Halloran's and my paternal grandmothers–Sarah and Mary–were sisters, and he and I are second cousins. Peggy also provided a copy of a brief history of the Halloran's lives in Ireland and Chicago, written by Joe Halloran in 1997. (Joe was a son of Patrick and Sarah (Joyce) Halloran and an uncle of Dan Halloran). **See Appendix Three, page 42.**

---

[22] The website, http://www.oidhreachtlca.ie, chronicles the history of Loughaconeera with documents and images.

Peggy Calhoun's tree includes genealogical records, displayed below and in **Appendix One, page 30,** from IrishGenealogy.ie for Mary Joyce and three of her siblings–Michael, John, and Sarah–showing birth dates, parental names of Bridget (Mary) O'Brien and Michael Joyce, and their birthplace of Loughaconeera.[23]  **See Appendix Four, page 46,** for a Genealogical Proof Argument supporting the Loughaconeera origin of Mary Joyce.

**Records for Mary Joyce and three of her siblings among the seven children of Bridget (O'Brien) Joyce and Michael Joyce**

| Child | Four birth, two baptismal, and one death record |
|---|---|
| Mary | **Birth:** 17 November 1872, **displayed below** |
| | **The following records are displayed in Appendix One, Administrative Records, page 30** |
| Michael | **Birth:** 05 August 1876; **baptism:** 03 Sept, 1876 |
| John | **Birth:** 13 April 1878; **baptism:** 20 May 1878; **death:** 11 February 1932 |
| Sarah | **Birth:** 7 May 1882 |

**Source for birth records: IrishGenealogy.ie**      **Source for baptismal records: RootsIreland.ie**

**17 November 1872 civil birth record of Mary Joyce**

An abbreviated Joyce/O'Brien family tree is displayed on the following page. I also verified and incorporated the Joyce line of Peggy's tree into my full Theobald/Kelly/McKelvey/Joyce family tree at https://www.ancestry.com/family-tree/tree/160255584?cfpid=282094565936is

---

[23] Civil and ecclesiastical events are recorded and filed in districts, not townlands like Loughaconeera. **Appendix One, page 30,** displays the names of Administrative Districts for Loughaconeera and Rosduff and six records listed in the table above.

# Abbreviated Joyce & O'Brien Family Tree

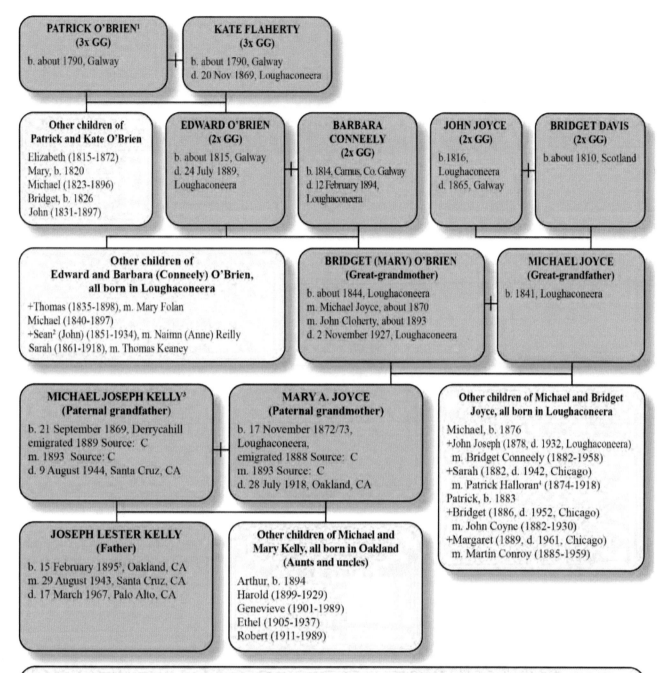

**PATRICK O'BRIEN[1]**
**(3x GG)**

b. about 1790, Galway

**KATE FLAHERTY**
**(3x GG)**

b. about 1790, Galway
d. 20 Nov 1869, Loughaconeera

**Other children of Patrick and Kate O'Brien**

Elizabeth (1815-1872)
Mary, b. 1820
Michael (1823-1896)
Bridget, b. 1826
John (1831-1897)

**EDWARD O'BRIEN**
**(2x GG)**

b. about 1815, Galway
d. 24 July 1889, Loughaconeera

**BARBARA CONNEELY**
**(2x GG)**

b. 1814, Camus, Co. Galway
d. 12 February 1894, Loughaconeera

**JOHN JOYCE**
**(2x GG)**

b. 1816, Loughaconeera
d. 1865, Galway

**BRIDGET DAVIS**
**(2x GG)**

b. about 1810, Scotland

**Other children of Edward and Barbara (Conneely) O'Brien, all born in Loughaconeera**

+Thomas (1835-1898), m. Mary Folan
Michael (1840-1897)
+Sean[2] (John) (1851-1934), m. Naimn (Anne) Reilly
Sarah (1861-1918), m. Thomas Keaney

**BRIDGET (MARY) O'BRIEN**
**(Great-grandmother)**

b. about 1844, Loughaconeera
m. Michael Joyce, about 1870
m. John Cloherty, about 1893
d. 2 November 1927, Loughaconeera

**MICHAEL JOYCE**
**(Great-grandfather)**

b. 1841, Loughaconeera

**MICHAEL JOSEPH KELLY[3]**
**(Paternal grandfather)**

b. 21 September 1869, Derrycahill
emigrated 1889 Source: C
m. 1893 Source: C
d. 9 August 1944, Santa Cruz, CA

**MARY A. JOYCE**
**(Paternal grandmother)**

b. 17 November 1872/73, Loughaconeera,
emigrated 1888 Source: C
m. 1893 Source: C
d. 28 July 1918, Oakland, CA

**Other children of Michael and Bridget Joyce, all born in Loughaconeera**

Michael, b. 1876
+John Joseph (1878, d. 1932, Loughaconeera)
  m. Bridget Conneely (1882-1958)
+Sarah (1882, d. 1942, Chicago)
  m. Patrick Halloran[4] (1874-1918)
Patrick, b. 1883
+Bridget (1886, d. 1952, Chicago)
  m. John Coyne (1882-1930)
+Margaret (1889, d. 1961, Chicago)
  m. Martin Conroy (1885-1959)

**JOSEPH LESTER KELLY**
**(Father)**

b. 15 February 1895[5], Oakland, CA
m. 29 August 1943, Santa Cruz, CA
d. 17 March 1967, Palo Alto, CA

**Other children of Michael and Mary Kelly, all born in Oakland (Aunts and uncles)**

Arthur, b. 1894
Harold (1899-1929)
Genevieve (1901-1989)
Ethel (1905-1937)
Robert (1911-1989)

---

See the full Joyce/O'Brien family tree at https://www.ancestry.com/family-tree/tree/160255584/family?cfpid=282094565936 with 264 people, 346 records, and 68 photos and other images.

+ I am a 2nd or 3rd cousin DNA match with one or more of their descendants of these six ancestors. Their parents are the Most Recent Common Ancestors of my DNA matches and me. See Appendix Four.

[1]The O'Briens may have come from Kilbride in County Mayo.

[2]Sean was an uncle of my grandmother, a father of nine children and scores of grandchildren, a farmer-fisherman, and a highly-regarded Gaelic storyteller.

[3]See the essay "Our Kelly Ancestors" for Michael Kelly's lineage and history.

[4]See Appendix Three for a brief history of Patrick Halloran's family.

[5]Our father's birth year is uncertain. His VA tombstone, WWII draft card, and Social Security death index show 1895. His CA death index and WWI draft card show 1894, and the 1900 U.S. Census shows 1896.

**Sources:** C above is the 1901 U.S. Federal Census. See the essay, "Our Joyce & O'Brien Ancestors," for dozens of additional sources.

**Researched and developed by Joyce Kelly, incorporating research findings and patrilines from Peggy Calhoun.**

**Our grandmother Mary (Joyce) Kelly, her husband/our grandfather Michael Kelly, and their six children**

Mary (Joyce) Kelly, c. 1900

Michael Kelly, c. 1943

Our father Joseph, 1917

Our father Joseph & Aunt Gene, c. 1901

Uncles Arthur (left) and Harry, c. 1902

Uncle Harry, c. 1925

Aunt Ethel, c. 1930

Aunt Gene, 1947

Uncle Bob, c. 1960

Thank you to Terrence Stauber for the photos of Mary, Joseph and Gene, and Harry; to Michael Coleman for the photo of Gene; to Jessi Kelly for the photo of Bob; and to my sister Julie for the other photos.

**Verification of the Joyce/O'Brien Family Tree with Genealogist David G. Riley's Research**

During this research, I saw several references to David Riley's unpublished papers, but I could not locate them until I contacted my DNA second cousin match, James Joyce. He also is a second cousin of David Riley and lent me his undated copy of Riley's "Descendants of Patrick O'Brien."

After Riley retired as a U.S. Navy Commander, he began researching Irish ancestors in Ireland and the U.S., decades before records were digitized. In both countries, Riley interviewed relatives, reviewed their family records, sought records in archives, and collaborated with other genealogists. Riley's 200-page manuscript on Patrick O'Brien's descendants consists of extensive family trees documenting a dozen Connemara families from 1790-2007, with nearly 1,000 chronological notes. Riley's notes summarize documents and interviews, but do not include copies of relevant records.

I compared my abbreviated Joyce/O'Brien family tree with Riley's excellent manuscript. In most instances, his and my conclusions are identical. However, neither of us obtained information about my great-grandfather Michael Joyce. Also, Riley's information and mine differ about my grandmother Mary (Joyce) Kelly. **See Appendix Two, page 34,** which displays nearly three dozen of Riley's excellent notes, independently verifying many entries in my family tree.

# 19th Century Ireland: Tenant Farmers, the Great Famine, and Emigration[24]

Our Joyce and O'Brien ancestors did not leave records and their lives were not chronicled by others because they were poor and illiterate. To understand what our ancestors' lives may have been like during the 19th century, this essay describes the general living conditions of poor Irish tenant farmers—**see Appendix Seven, page 71.**

After England conquered Ireland in 1601, the Crown confiscated land from native Irish Catholics and awarded it to Anglicans. The Crown awarded vast tracts to the English gentry and smaller tracts to English and Scottish settlers and conquering English soldiers. This process, and the 1649 Penal Laws,[25] reduced landowning Irish Catholics to tenants, who leased small plots of land on large estates owned by English or Anglo-Irish landlords. By 1778, Irish Catholics owned 5% of Irish land and the average Irish family leased less than ten acres. During the 1841 Census, 40% of Irish farmers lived in one-room cottages without windows or chimneys that they built themselves. Up to a dozen family members lived in one room, slept in straw on the dirt floor, and shared the space with the family's pigs and chickens.

---

[24] Sources include: *A Statistical and Agricultural Survey of the County of Galway* by Hely Dutton, University Press, Dublin, 1824; *Irish Peasants - Violence and Political Unrest,* 1780-1914, edited by Samuel Clark & James S. Donneelly, Jr., University of Wisconsin Press, 1983; and other materials listed below.

[25] The Penal Laws in 1649 disenfranchised the native Catholic majority from religious, cultural, political, social, and economic freedom. Catholics could not send their children to school; practice their religion; vote; hold office; or own land, a business, or property. All Irish culture, music, and education was banned. To avoid these sanctions, many Anglo-Irish leaders converted to the Anglican Church, depriving Catholic peasants of the leadership needed to regain their rights, and, later, to survive the Great Famine. Penal Laws were finally revoked in the late 19th century.

Tenant farmers in Ireland could be evicted at any time. By law, any improvements tenants made to the house or land became the property of the landlord. Therefore, tenants rarely improved their cottages and land. Some landlords and their agents were ruthless, causing their tenants to live in a permanent state of insecurity about possible eviction or increased rent. Landlords generally lived elsewhere and hired agents who regularly subdivided holdings while increasing rents.

Families relied on potatoes for food and income. By 1800, most Irish farmers ate only potatoes, which are remarkably nutritious and easy to grow in Ireland's cool moist soil. One acre of fertilized soil could yield up 12 tons of potatoes, enough to feed a family of six and their animals for a year. But, primitive agricultural practices, bad weather, and blight reduced productivity, leading to hunger, starvation, and emigration. Diseases such as scurvy and typhus were common while Ireland exported grain, corn, and meat, primarily to England. Meanwhile, the population continued to increase, creating a labor surplus—landlords and middlemen responded by raising rents and decreasing wages. By 1845, on the eve of the Great Famine (called "Great Hunger" in Ireland), landless laborers and farmers with fewer than 20 acres accounted for over 75 percent of all farmers.

Western Galway was populated by large families of Catholic tenants who were Irish speaking and extremely poor. The land was rocky and poorly suited to large farms. Wet weather annually threatened crops. Most families had small gardens, kept livestock, and traveled by donkey and cart. In villages on the coast, like Loughaconeera and Rosmuc, men and their families were farmer-fishermen, supplementing their diet of potatoes with fish.

Paying high rents, mandatory tithes to the Anglican Church of Ireland, and surviving on potatoes for their food and livelihood, the Irish population was vulnerable to famine. Finally, a series of failed potato harvests, between 1845-1852, led to the Great Famine, causing a million farmers to die from disease and starvation and more than a million to emigrate. Throughout Ireland, entire communities disappeared. Most of our ancestors emigrated in the late 19th century, after surviving the Great Famine. Essays on the next two pages, by a local Irish historian and a mid-19th century American visitor to Ireland, describe the catastrophic Great Famine.

**Cottage interior, 1846**   **Digging potatoes, c. 1900**   **Gathering seaweed, c. 1900**

*Interior of a peasant's cottage.*
Pictorial Times 1846

**The Great Potato Famine of 1845-1852,[26] described in 2006 by Historian Tim Robinson**

"'Three hundred and sixty-five days of the year we have the potato. Because the landowner sees we can live and work hard on 'em, he grinds us down in our wages, and then despises us because we are ignorant and ragged.' So spoke a seaweed-gatherer in 1845, to Asenath Nicholson of New York, who was walking around Ireland reading the gospel to anyone who would listen.

"...Potato blight, a fungal disease new to Europe, was first noticed in Belgium in June 1845. The infection fell on the leaves of flourishing plants and rioted in the tubers. Soon an offensive smell was perceptible in the fields, and when the potatoes were dug, they were found to be black sacs of putridity. Throughout Ireland about half the year's crop was lost. And, especially in the West, where wheat could not be grown, there was little else to eat. ...the 1846 crop was totally destroyed by the blight. The following year, 'Black Forty-seven,' had a long bitter winter and the onslaught of fever... people were too enfeebled by malnourishment to till the land. In the first half of 1849, cholera followed upon starvation... and by degrees the crisis subsided into decades of chronic deprivation. ...the Famine was the keystone in a triumphal arch of suffering. And for long after the worst years of hunger, the survivors were further bereaved by mass emigration.

"The Commissioners of Works reported that 'fishermen, weakened in body from want of food, are reluctant to undergo increased exertion which severe weather unavoidably requires, and which, from the wretched nature of their equipment, is inevitable.... Crimes of survival such as sheep-stealing filled the prison in Clifden with what its keeper described as 'half starved, half naked beings in human form...the population of the Clifden Union (where Loughaconeera is located) decreased by 27 percent from 1841 to 1851.... I suspect that death carried off most, for death demands less effort from exhausted bodies, less hope, and less cash, than emigration. Over the succeeding years, many more, weakened and desolated by the Famine, followed them into death or exile. Others survived, half-forgot the past, sang the old songs again, and even prospered. The Famine was just a period, and Time turned its back on the victims as soon as they were dead.

"During the months I spent walking the rocky shores, windy hillsides and briar-tangled boreens of Connemara while making my map, I was shown so many famine graves that I ceased, out of discouragement, to record them all. It was a failing. And despite all my imaginings of voices to be recaptured from them, there is nobody in those graves to hear my apology for it.

"A pattern of depopulation and emigration continued well into the 20th century as Irish people left the west of Ireland for a better life in America, Britain and further afield. In the latter half of the 19th century, the Land League and the Irish Parliamentary Party campaigned for the rights of tenant farmers. By the turn of the 20th century, a series of land acts had been passed securing the

---

[26] This text is quoted from *Listening to the Wind, The Connemara Trilogy, Part One*, by Tim Robinson, Penguin Books, 2006, pp.187-202. Robinson (1935-2020) was an Irish cartographer, historian, geologist, and resident of Roundstone, 18 miles west of Loughaconeera.

rights of tenants, the landlord system was broken up and most Irish farmers had been able to purchase their land. But farms generally were small and not sufficiently productive to support large families, typically causing all children but a single son (who stayed home to care for his parents and the farm) to emigrate." (End of excerpt).

> **British policies in 19ᵗʰ century Ireland[27] forced a million poor Irish farmers to emigrate due to the lack of religious freedom, land ownership, food, legal and political rights, and opportunities.**
>
> The population of Ireland decreased from 8,180,000 in 1841 to 4,460,000 in 1901. Massive emigration affected every corner of the country, including among our Joyce and O'Brien ancestors. After the Famine, five of Mary Joyce's six brothers and sisters emigrated to America (brother Patrick remained on the family farm; brother John emigrated but returned to Ireland after having an accident in Chicago).
>
> A mid-19th century memoir[28] describes a common landlord/tenant relationship that forced tenants to emigrate. "Two miles from the town (in Connemara) a decently clad farmer accosted me. He had been to attend a lawsuit, a case of ejectment. 'I have worked,' he said, 'on this farm since I was a boy; my father died, and left it to me, three years ago. I had made a comfortable house for myself and my family and been preparing manure all winter to put in a greater crop of potatoes and corn. The agent came round, saw the improvements, and told me I should not sow any seed, but must quit the premises.'
>
> "He actually was ejected, notwithstanding the encouragement he had from the landlord to make improvements. 'I must take my little all,' added the man, 'and leave my father's bones, and seek a home in America.' Hard is the lot of the poor man in Ireland. If he is industrious, his industry will not secure him a home and its comforts; these he must lose so soon as this home is above the abode of the ox or ass…. These are the facts all over Ireland. If the poor tenant improves the premises, he must be turned out or pay more. If he does not improve it, he is a lazy dirty Irishman, and must be put out for that."
>
> **Source:** *Ireland's Welcome to the Stranger*, Asenath Nicholson, Baker and Scribner, 1847, page 391.
> See **Appendix Seven, page 71,** for more information on mid-19ᵗʰ century evictions in Ireland.

### After the Great Potato Famine

During and immediately after the Famine, our ancestors remained on their farms; tending children, livestock, house and garden; harvesting seaweed and turf; and fishing. They continued living in Loughaconeera until 1882, when Sara O'Brien, a sister of our great-grandmother Bridget Mary (O'Brien) Joyce, emigrated to Chicago—a city that attracted many immigrants from Rosmuc.

---

[27] Fully addressing the relationship between Ireland and England is beyond the scope of this family history.

[28] During 1844-45, Asenath Nicholson, a pious American, walked around Ireland distributing religious tracts and bibles to the poor, and investigating their conditions. Her book, *Ireland's Welcome to the Stranger*, details her observations. At the time, many landowners, their agents, and tourists described the Irish as "barely human" and most tourists stayed in the "Big Houses" of wealthy English and Anglo-Irish landowners. Nicholson stayed with poor farmers to whom she provided religious books, a sympathetic ear, and small payments for food and lodging.

By the end of the 19ᵗʰ century, the last Penal Laws were repealed, mandatory tithes to the Anglican Church were abolished, and Catholic Emancipation was won. Meanwhile, as industrialization brought growth and prosperity to cities throughout Europe, lack of industry in Galway City caused its population to decline. The population of County Galway peaked at 422,923 before the Great Famine and collapsed to 182,244 in 1911. County Galway was in serious economic and social decline, with small-farm agriculture the main economic activity.

At the same time, the artisan fishing industry throughout Galway collapsed following the arrival of large steam-powered trawlers from elsewhere. Due to rapidly declining opportunities at home, all but one of the next generation of seven Joyce/O'Brien children–our grandmother and her siblings–left Loughaconeera as young adults and emigrated to Chicago. Our grandmother was an exception, settling in Oakland, California, where her future husband arrived a year later.

**Residents of a typical Irish village in the late 19ᵗʰ and early 20ᵗʰ centuries**

**Tending the fire and spinning wool in an Irish village, County Donegal, 1880-1900**

**The Effects of the Great Potato Famine and Emigration on the Population of Irish Speakers**

The map below shows the proportion of residents in each county who spoke Irish in 1871 as more than 50% (red), 25-50% (dark pink), and 0-25% (light pink).[29] County Galway was mainly red– one of the most traditional counties in Ireland. Note the white Anglicized east, central, and north, except for County Donegal.

In 1800, there were about four million Irish speakers, and bilingualism was common except in the eastern counties and in the West, where many Irish speakers were monolingual. But because English fluency was considered essential, teaching in Irish was prohibited in National Schools from their founding in 1831 until 1871. The number of Irish speakers further declined during the Potato Famine, 1845-1849, when disease and mass starvation disproportionately took the lives of Irish-speaking potato farmers. Finally, up to one million Irish, many from the Irish-speaking West, emigrated during the 19th and early 20th centuries.

Throughout Ireland, the percent of the population who spoke Irish, by decade born, declined from 45% for those born during the decade beginning in 1771 to 13% for those born during the decade beginning in 1861. In the county of Galway, where the Irish language was more prevalent, the proportion of Irish speakers declined from 91% to 56% during that same period, according to Garrett Fitzgerald, *Prevalence of Irish Speakers*, Royal Irish Academy, vol.84c, 1984, p. 117. See the map on the following page.

**Irish villagers in the late 19th and early 20th centuries**

---

[29] The term 'Gaeltacht' describes areas of Ireland, primarily in the West, where the Irish language is more common than English. This is partly due to young, English-speaking residents migrating to urban areas in Ireland and abroad.

**Prevalence of Irish speakers in 1871**

**Red=>50%; dark pink=25-50%; light pink=0-25% white=0**

**Source:** E.G. Ravenstein, Prevalence of Celtic Languages in 1871,
*Journal of the Statistical Society of London*, September 1879, p. 583.

## Locations of Joyce Ancestors' Farms in Loughaconeera, County Galway

The 1670 Down Survey is the earliest surviving Irish land survey, extending back to 1641. At that time, Loughaconeera's name was Slewkiroggy, with Catholic owners Thomas McRedmund Joyce and Murrogh McDow Flaherty. Other owners were the Protestant College of Dublin and Maurice Thompson, and Catholic Richard Martin. Later Loughaconeera surveys include the 1823-1837 Tithe Valuation and Applotment; and the 1842 Valuation showing 11 houses. Griffith's Valuation was the first survey to list tenants' names. The Loughaconeera Heritage website describes these land surveys at http://www.oidhreachtlca.ie/19th-century.php.

Griffith's Valuation, conducted throughout Ireland during the mid-1800s, evaluated property to establish a "rateable" (taxable) value to fund workhouses during the Great Famine. Loughaconeera's GV listing (below) shows that 12 tenants, including Patrick and John Joyce, leased property from immediate lessor Nicholas Lynch[30] in 1857. Our 2x great-grandfather John Joyce (b. 1816) was 41 years old and his son Patrick (b. 1841) was 16 years old. They likely were the tenants with adjacent properties listed below. Our great-grandfather Michael (b.1845) was only 12 years old and therefore would not have had a separate tenancy.

---

[30] **Appendix Eight, page 74**, discusses Nicholas Lynch and his son Marcus who owned Loughaconeera and seven adjacent townlands. They resided in a "Big House" in Barna, just west of Galway City.

**Loughaconeera Farms, County Galway, c. 2010**

**Griffith's Valuation (GV) for Property in Loughaconeera, 1857, Guide by Column:** 1st= property designation; 2nd=occupier; 3rd=immediate lessor; 4th=description (offices were farm buildings); 5th=acreage; 6th through 8th=taxable value, in pounds, shillings, and pence, expressed as the annual potential income of each family's land (col. 6), buildings (col. 7) and total (col. 8).

| 1 | 2 | 3 | 4 | 5 | 6 | 7 | 8 |
|---|---|---|---|---|---|---|---|
| | LOUGHACONEERA. (Ord. S. 64 & 65.) | | | | | | |
| a | John Hernan, . | | House, offices, & land, | | 2 0 0 | 0 15 0 | 2 15 0 |
| b | Mary Greelash, . | | House, offices, & land, | | 4 0 0 | 0 10 0 | 4 10 0 |
| c | Patrick Dundas, | | House, offices, & land, | | 2 15 0 | 0 12 0 | 3 7 0 |
| d | Colman M'Donough, | | House, offices, & land, | | 1 15 0 | 0 10 0 | 2 5 0 |
| e | Patrick Sullivan, | | House, offices, & land, | | 3 8 0 | 0 10 0 | 3 18 0 |
| f | John M'Donough, | | House and land, | | 1 15 0 | 0 3 0 | 1 18 0 |
| g | Patrick Joyce, | Nicholas Lynch, | House, office, & land, | 1380 3 29 | 1 17 0 | 0 4 0 | 2 1 0 |
| h | John Joyce, . | | House, offices, & land. | | 1 15 0 | 0 5 0 | 2 0 0 |
| i | Martin Walsh, sen., & Mn. Walsh, jun. | | House, office, & land, | | 1 0 0 / 1 0 0 | 0 5 0 | 2 5 0 |
| j | William Hanrahan, | | House, office, & land, | | 1 0 0 | 0 5 0 | 1 5 0 |
| k | John Kearney, . | | House, offices, & land, | | 2 0 0 | 0 8 0 | 2 8 0 |
| l | Colman Sullivan, . | Martin Walsh, sen,, . | House, office, & land, | | 1 0 0 | 0 4 0 | 1 4 0 |
| | | | Water, . . . | 47 2 37 | — | — | — |
| | | | Total, . . | 1434 2 26 | 25 5 0 | 4 11 0 | 29 16 0 |

**Tenants' total land area** (col. 5) is shown as 1380 acres (more than two square miles)—averaging 115 acres per tenant family, but much was not suitable for farming due to rocky soil and proximity to the sea. (The record shows that 47 acres were covered by water.) At the time, most Irish tenant farmers leased 5 to 30 acres. The average Loughaconeera farmer's building value was 7 shillings. Buildings at the bottom of the GV property scale, of 15 shillings or less, typically were one or two room clay cabins with a thatch or turf roof.

In 1869, twelve years after Griffith's' Valuation, Marcus Lynch, the son of Nicholas Lynch (the lessor on GV), put up for auction his estate of eight lots of 9,565 acres, running along the coast for about eight miles. (**See Appendix Eight, page 74, for a discussion of the Lynch family.**) Lot 7 was Loughaconeera. The sales announcement included a list of current (1869) tenants and an 1857 GV map for each of the eight townlands. The sales announcement (below, right) mentions that "tenants are yearly and hold at low rents, the letting having been made about 20 years ago," suggesting that the Lynches were "good" landlords. The announcement also notes that "upwards of 7,000 pounds has been laid out in improvements …and new owners could "increase the Rental considerably." I learned that all but two lots sold, but I could not locate information about tenants' subsequent rental arrangements and livelihoods.

**1869 auction of Marcus Lynch's estate of eight lots of 9,565 acres in Moyrus Civil Parish[31]**

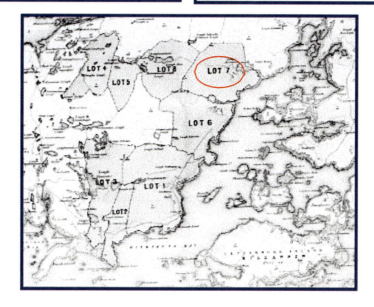

---

[31] This information is from http://www.oidhreachtlca.ie/index.php. Click on "Galleries," then "Sale 1869."

Several of 12 GV households in 1857 remained in 1869 on Lot 7, Loughaconeera. Our great grand-uncle **Patrick Joyce** remained but his father John had died in 1865. **Edward O'Brien**, our 2x great-grandfather, was a tenant in 1869 but not in 1857. Joyces also leased land in other lots/townlands (not displayed here) on Lynch's estate, including Michael Joyce (possibly my great-grandfather) on Lot 1 in Kilkieran; Thomas Joyce, Lot 2, Ardmore, plus 530 acres in Lot 5, Shaunodonnnell; and Patrick Joyce, Barbara Joyce, and Martin Joyce, Lot 6, Kylesalia.

**1869 list of 18 tenants for Lot 7, Loughaconeera**

| No | Denomination | Tenants' Names | Quantity of Land Statute Measure a r p | Yearly Rent. £ s d |
|---|---|---|---|---|
| 1 | LOUGHACONNEERA, Situate in the Barony of Ballinahinch, and County of Galway. | In Owners hands, | — 55 3 27 | — |
| 2 | | Thomas Beatty, | — 3 1 0 | 1 0 0 |
| 3 | | Patrick Joyce, | — 9 3 38 | 2 17 8 |
| 4 | | Widow Coyne, | — 12 3 16 | 3 8 4 |
| 5 | | John Lally, | — 7 2 5 | 2 12 0 |
| 6 | | John Folan, | — 14 3 15 | 3 13 6 |
| 7 | | Edward O'Brien, | — 16 1 39 | 4 4 0 |
| 8 | | Dudley Sullivan, | — 24 2 18 | 4 14 6 |
| 9 | | Patrick Dundas, | — 23 3 5 | 1 3 0 |
| 10 | | John Kearney, | — 15 3 30 | 3 3 0 |
| 11 | | Patrick Gearey, | — 16 1 29 | 4 9 4 |
| 12 | | Peter Conneely, | — 15 0 6 | 4 4 0 |
| 13 | | John Sullivan, | — 6 3 18 | 1 0 0 |
| 14 | | John Hernon, | — 20 1 1 | 4 5 0 |
| 15 | | Peter Kelly, | — 12 1 10 | 1 0 0 |

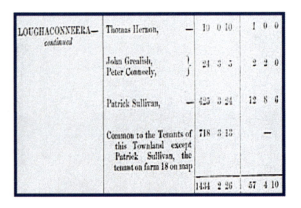

| | | | Quantity a r p | Rent £ s d |
|---|---|---|---|---|
| LOUGHACONNEERA— *continued* | Thomas Hernon, | | — 19 0 10 | 1 0 0 |
| | John Grealish, Peter Conneely, | } | 24 3 5 | 2 2 0 |
| | Patrick Sullivan, | | — 425 3 24 | 12 6 6 |
| | Common to the Tenants of this Townland except Patrick Sullivan, the tenant on farm 18 on map | | 718 3 13 | — |
| | | | 1434 2 26 | 57 4 10 |

**Griffiths Valuation map of Loughaconeera, 1857**

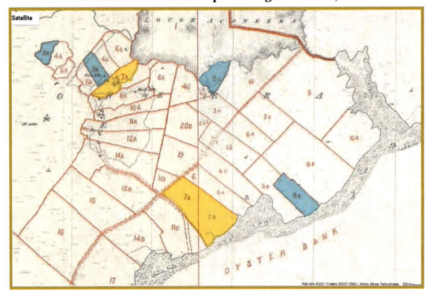

**Source:** www.askaboutireland.ie/griffith-valuation/

24

**Ordnance Survey of Ireland, Geohive map of Loughaconeera, undated, but likely mid-19ᵗʰ century**

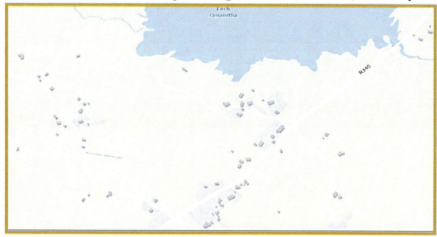

**Satellite view of Loughaconeera on Google maps, 2021**

## Select Joyce Family Records and Irish Census Data, 1901-1952

The 1901 Census showed 26 households in Loughaconeera, with a total of 153 residents, all Roman Catholic. Mary Joyce had emigrated to America thirteen years earlier, and her mother Bridget was living with her second husband, John Cloherty, and her remaining children (top of next page). Bridget's first husband, Michael Joyce, likely died before then, although there is no civil death or burial record in the Clifden registration district.[32] On the 1911 Census (page 27), Bridget and John lived alone and reported being married for 18 years, indicating a marriage year of 1893, although we found no record to corroborate this. Additional Joyce family records are displayed below and in Appendix One, page 30.

---

[32] It seems odd that neither David G. Riley nor I could locate any information about Michael Joyce. While searching for him, I located the record of a merchant seaman named Michael Joyce who died in England about this time but could not verify that he was "our" Michael Joyce.

**1901 Census of Ireland, Loughaconeera, house #14**

Columns show relation to head, religion, literacy, age, gender, position, marriage status, birthplace, and languages.

| # | | | | | | | | | | | |
|---|---|---|---|---|---|---|---|---|---|---|---|
| 1 | John | Cloherty | Rip. Head | Roman Catholic | Cannot Read | 44 | - | M | Farmer | Married | Co Galway | Irish & English |
| 2 | Bridget | Cloherty | Wife | Roman Catholic | Cannot Read | 40 | | F | | Married | Co Galway | Irish |
| 3 | Audley | Cloherty | Son | Roman Catholic | Read & Write | 16 | | M | Farmer's Son | not married | Co Galway | Irish & English |
| 4 | Michael | Joyce | Step-son | Roman Catholic | Read & Write | 23 | | M | Farmer's Son | not married | Co Galway | Irish & English |
| 5 | John | Joyce | Step-son | Roman Catholic | Read & Write | 20 | | M | Farmer's Son | not married | Co Galway | Irish & English |
| 6 | Patrick | Joyce | Step-son | Roman Catholic | Read & Write | 18 | | M | Farmer's Son | not married | Co Galway | Irish & English |
| 7 | Sarah | Joyce | Step-daughter | Roman Catholic | Read & Write | 16 | | F | Farmer's Daughter | not married | Co Galway | Irish & English |
| 8 | Bridget | Joyce | Step-daughter | Roman Catholic | Read & Write | 14 | | F | Farmer's Daughter | not married | Co Galway | Irish & English |
| 9 | Margaret | Joyce | Step-daughter | Roman Catholic | Read & Write | 12 | | F | Scholar | not married | Co Galway | Irish & English |

**Source: National Archives of Ireland**

**Loughaconeera's population reflected high birth and emigration rates**

| | |
|---|---|
| 1857 Griffith's Valuation | 12 households |
| 1869 Sale of Townland | 18 households |
| 1901 Census | 26 households, 153 residents |
| 1911 Census | 32 households, 156 residents |
| 2011 Census | 27 households, 65 residents |
| 2017 Census | 51 residents |

The number of households in Loughaconeera increased from 12 in 1857 to 26 in 1901. Between 1901 and 1911, there were six additional households. but only three additional residents, reflecting the emigration of young people, primarily to America. By 2011, there were only 65 residents, representing a 58% population loss over the previous century. By 2017, there were 51 residents.

Mary Joyce emigrated to America in 1888 when she was nearly 16 and settled in Oakland, perhaps because her future husband, Michael Kelly, had family there. Later, Mary's sisters–Sarah, Bridget, and Margaret–settled in Chicago.[33] That city and Boston were the most popular destinations for Irish immigrants from Connemara. Beginning in 1900, U.S. immigration collected the destinations of immigrants and the names of sponsors who paid the ship's fare. Mary's sister, Bridget, reported their aunt, Mrs. Sarah Keaney, at 131 East Superior Street in Chicago, as destination and payor.

---

[33] **See Appendix Two, page 34,** "Verification of my Joyce/O'Brien Family Tree with David G. Riley's Research," for information on the immigration of Mary's three sisters. See **Appendix Three, page 42,** "Halloran Family History," for a description of their lives in Chicago.

**Margaret Joyce (Mary's sister) married Martin Conroy on 27 April 1910**

The certificate lists Margaret's parents as **Michael Joyce and Bridget O'Brien.**

Arch Diœcesis Chic.

| Nomen Familiæ. | A. D., Die Mensis. | REGISTRUM MATRIMONIORUM. | Dispen. |
|---|---|---|---|
| Conroy and Joyce | Die April 27. 1910 | Ego infrascriptus, ad hoc officium invitatus ac rogatus, nec vi aut gravi metu constrictus, ... missis ... denuntiationibus, et mutuo contrahentium consensu habito per verba de præsenti, matrimonio conjunxi Martinum Conroy e loco 1342 C Portland Ave Chicago Filium Michaelem Conroy Brigittam Coyne baptizatum in ... die ... mensis ... Anni ... cujus de statu libero satis constabat et Margaritam Joyce e loco 1342 Cleveland Ave Chic. Filiam Michaelem Joyce Brigittam O'Brien baptizatam in ... die ... mensis ... Anni ... in hac parochia, per ... mens ... (Vel) ann aliquot Commorantem. Præsentibus testibus Johanne Coyne et Brigitta Coyne. Hujus Matrimonii notitiam ... ad Registra ecclesiarum in quibus praedicti Sponsi baptizati sunt. P. J. Scanlan Pastor (aut) delegatus a Sponso {Parocho Ordinario | |

Date: 27 Apr 1910

Place: Chicago, Cook County, Illinois

Description: Marriage of Margaret Joyce to Martin Conroy

Transcription: document indicating parents of each: Michael Conroy and Bridget Coyne; Michael Joyce and Bridget O'Brien. In the presence of Margaret Joyce's sister Bridget and Bridget's husband John Coyne

**Source:** Ancestry.com

**John and Bridget (O'Brien) Joyce Cloherty lived alone during the 1911 Census**

Residents of a house 1 in Loughaconeera (Owangowla, Galway)

Show all information

| Surname | Forename | Age | Sex | Relation to head | Religion |
|---|---|---|---|---|---|
| Cloherty | John | 71 | Male | Head of Family | Roman Catholic |
| Cloherty | Bridget | 67 | Female | Wife | Roman Catholic |

By 1911, six of Bridget's seven children had emigrated to the U.S. Her son John and his family returned to Loughaconeera after he had an accident in Chicago. Patrick did not emigrate and he was present when his mother died in 1927.

**In 1927, Mary's mother, Bridget, died in Loughaconeera. Her son Patrick was present**

| | | | | | | | | | |
|---|---|---|---|---|---|---|---|---|---|
| 19 27 Second November Loughaconeera Clifden N. D. | Bridget Cloherty | F | married | 84 years | Wife of a Farmer | Old age and Debility No medical Attendant | Pat Joyce Present at death Loughconeera | Tenth November 19 27 | M. E. O'Connor Registrar. |

Finally, a 27 September 1952 obituary in the *Chicago Tribune* for Bridget (Joyce) Coyne, listed her sisters Mary Kelly and Sarah Halloran, parents Michael Joyce and Bridget O'Brien, and uncle Sean O'Brien of Loughaconeera. These ancestors are listed on the Joyce/O'Brien family tree on page 13, convincing Peggy Calhoun and me that our Mary Joyces were the same person.

**Bridget Joyce Coyne's Obituary, which refers to Mary Kelly**

COYNE - Bridget **Joyce** Coyne, Sept. 27, 1952, beloved wife of the late John Coyne, mother of Martin, Mary, Catherine **Kotor**, Margaret **McGee**, Alyce **Doyle**, and the late Patrick and Sarah Coyne, sister of Margaret **Conroy** and the late Michael, John, and Patrick Joyce, Mary **Kelly** and Sarah **Halloran**. Funeral Wednesday, 9:30 a.m., from funeral home, 245 W. North avenue, to Immaculate Conception church. Interment Mount Carmel. *[date of birth: 15 Aug 1886] [date of death: 27 Sep 1952] [ Bridget is the daughter of Michael **Joyce** & Bridget **O'Brien** and a niece of Seán O'Brien of Loughaconeera, Carna ]*

**Many Irish in Ireland and America embraced ballads and poems to express the remorse and nostalgia associated with massive emigration during the 19ᵗʰ century.**

### My Connemara

Lake, sea, land and sky,
Overall, a glancing eye,
Bog, plain and mountains high,
Heaven now seems almost nigh!

Cottages, cairns, and coral sands,
All welcoming like outstretched hands,
Castles too, with history filled,
Their gardens scented, air distilled.

Monuments to an age gone-by,
Spectacular against the sky,
Fisher-folk who know the sea,
Yet view with awe its rocky lea.

It's pathways, boreens, sounds of sheep,
A picture in my mind to keep!

Margaret Mitchell, in *The Way It Was,* edited by Paul Gannon, Ashford Press, 1999, p. 378.

Mitchell (1900-1949), an Irish American, wrote the Pulitzer prize-winning novel, *Gone with the Wind.*

# Acknowledgements

This essay was a group accomplishment–I'm grateful to many people. In 1994, my sister Julie obtained Mary's death certificate, visited her grave in Oakland, and contacted relatives to learn about our grandparents, but those with information were deceased. In 2018, Jim became curious and began researching the genealogy of our grandparents. Jim invited me to work with him the following year. My sister Kate sought, but could not locate, the record of Mary's marriage.

We identified Mary Joyce's ancestral home in Ireland because Dan Halloran and I tested on FamilyTreeDNA, revealing a second cousin relationship but we could not identify a common ancestor. Later, while seeking information on my match with Joe Kelly (for our Kelly line), I emailed Noel Murphy, Joe's contact person. Noel told me that Joe lived in the Rosmuc area of Ireland and he suggested that I join the Rosmuc Area Genealogy and DNA Facebook Group that he co-founded. Noel also ran GEDmatch kits for my brother, sisters, and me with Matchmaker to search for additional matches with Rosmuc Group members. Noel contacted me about my close matches with several kits managed by Peggy Calhoun in the Rosmuc Group.

Shortly after I posted Matchmaker results to the Facebook Group, Peggy Calhoun contacted me. My DNA matches with her relatives, including her second cousin, Dan Halloran, persuaded Peggy that my Mary Joyce likely was related to her cousins in Rosmuc and Loughaconeera. After Peggy shared her family tree and records, I completed a preliminary Joyce & O'Brien line back to 1771. Around that same time, I contacted Jim Joyce, another Ancestry DNA second cousin. Jim identified his paternal grandfather as John Joseph Joyce, born in Loughaconeera. Peggy's tree showed that Dan's paternal grandmother, Jim's paternal grandfather, and my paternal grandmother, Mary Joyce, were siblings, born in Loughaconeera.

I also hired genealogists, a graphic artist, a translator and an expert in Word. Clare Doyle, founder of Wild Atlantic Way in County Galway, searched local records for our Joyce line. Terri Stern, founder of My Genealogy Tutor, uploaded DNA test results for the four of us siblings to GEDmatch; conducted analyses described in Appendix Four, the Genealogical Proof Argument; and taught me the DNA analytic skills displayed in this essay. Readers of the draft essay who provided helpful comments include my brother and sisters, Jim Hollarn and Noel Murphy, co-founders of the Rosmuc Group, Michelle Leonard, founder of Genes and Genealogy, and Elaine Andrews, a long-time friend, author and editor.

Ken Falk of Ken Falk Marketing and Communications designed the cover and abbreviated Joyce/O'Brien family tree. Bridget Anne Hughes translated from Irish to English folktales by Sean O'Briain. And she located and translated a song about the landowners of Loughaconeera. Erin Gilday applied her formidable Word skills to help prepare the manuscript for printing.

Finally, I thank my husband Paul Healey for his patience, funny jokes, and support (including planning, shopping, and cooking our delicious daily dinners), while I focused intently for several years on researching the family histories of our four grandparents.

# Appendix One

## Administrative Districts for
## Loughaconeera (Lough Con Aortha) and Rosduff (Ros Dubh)

-

Ireland has four provinces and 32 counties. Before emigrating to America, our Joyce ancestors lived in County Galway and our Kelly ancestors lived in County Roscommon-both in the Province of Connaught. Our McKelvey ancestors lived in County Donegal in the Province of Ulster.

**Local Administrative Districts**

The Joyces, O'Briens, and their ancestors lived in Loughaconeera from before 1816 until after 1927. Similarly, the Hallorans and their ancestors lived in Rosduff in the Rosmuc Parish/Peninsula, since at least that same time. Although Loughaconeera and Rosduff are separated by only four miles across the Bay or six miles on roads, they are in different administrative districts.

Before locating records, it's necessary to identify the administrative district for each type of record. For example, census records are maintained by Townland within District Electoral Divisions. Thus, census records for Loughaconeera can be found under the Owengowla DED, then under the Townland of Loughaconeera in Owengowla. In contrast, birth records for Loughaconeera are categorized under the Civil Parish of Moyrus and under the Civil Registration District of Clifden, then under Loughaconeera within Moyrus or Clifden. Civil records from Rosduff are recorded in the Townland/DED of Turlough. See the table and maps below.

## Administrative Districts in West County Galway with records for Joyces and Hallorans

| Townland (the smallest administrative unit) | Loughaconeera is a Townland | Rosduff is a village in the Townland of Turlough |
|---|---|---|
| Parliamentary Division | Connemara | Connemara |
| Barony | Ballynahinch | Moycullen |
| Civil Parish* | Moyrus | Kilcummin |
| Roman Catholic Parish* | Moyrus or Carna[34] | Rosmuc |
| District Electoral Division* | Owengowla | Turlough |
| Civil Registration District/Poor Law Union * | Clifden | Oughterard |
| Constabulary District | Roundstone | Oughterard |
| Peninsula | Iorras Ainbhtheach (or Aithneach) | Rosmuc[35] |

*Maps show geographic areas and boundaries.

**Civil Registration Districts/Poor Law Unions**

**Civil Parishes (CPs)**

61=Kilcummin CP includes Rosmuc Peninsula; 109=Moyrus CP includes Loughaconeera

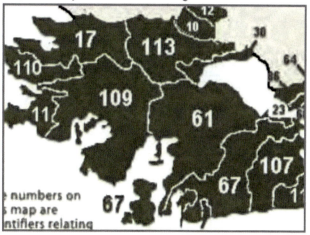

**Source of six maps:** www.johngrenham.com

---

[34] Residents of Loughaconeera likely worshipped at St. Kieran's Church in Kilkieran – a journey of less than four miles. In 1842, St. Mary's Catholic Church was built in Carna - 10 miles from Loughaconeera.

[35] Rosmuc also is the name of a townland on the peninsula. Rosmuc townland is several miles south of Rosduff.

| **Roman Catholic Parishes** | **Owengowla Elect. Div. includes Loughaconeera** |
|---|---|

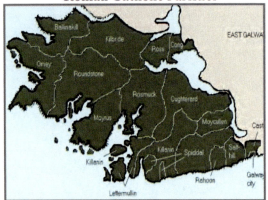 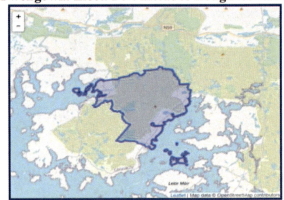

| **Turlough Elect. Div. includes Rosmuc Peninsula** | **Turlough Townland includes Rosduff** |
|---|---|

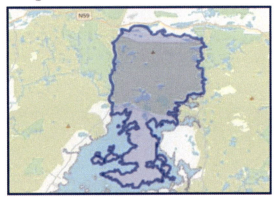 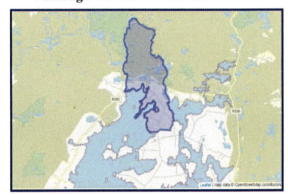

**Birth, baptismal and death records for Mary Joyce and three of her siblings among the seven children of Bridget (O'Brien) Joyce and Michael Joyce**

| Child | Birth, baptismal, and death records |
|---|---|
| Mary | **Birth:** 17 November 1872/73 **(displayed on page 12)** |
| Michael | **Birth:** 05 August 1876; **baptism:** 03 Sept, 1876 |
| John | **Birth:** 13 April 1878; **baptism:** 20 May 1878; **death:** 11 February 1932 |
| Sarah | **Birth:** 7 May 1882 |

Source for birth records: IrishGenealogy.ie          Source for baptismal records: RootsIreland.ie

**5 August 1876 civil birth record of Mary Joyce's brother, Michael Joyce**

| 361 | Fifth August 18 76 Loughconera | Michael | M | Michael Joyce Loughconera | Bridget Joyce formerly O'Brien | Farmer | John O'Brien his mark Present at birth Loughconera | Fourth September 18 76 | a B Reamer |

**3 September 1876 baptismal record of Mary Joyce's brother, Michael Joyce**

| Name: | Michael Joyce | Date of Birth: | |
| | | Date of Baptism: | 03-Sep-1876 |
| Address: | Loughconniere | Parish/District: | CARNA |
| Gender: | Male | County | Co. Galway |
| | | Denomination: | Roman Catholic |
| Father: | Michael Joyce | Mother: | Bridget O'Brien |
| Occupation: | | | |
| Sponsor 1 / Informant 1: | John O'Brien | Sponsor 2 / Informant 2: | Barbara Connealy |

**13 April 1878 civil birth record of Mary Joyce's brother, John Joyce**

| Thirtieth April 1878 Loughconera | John | M | Michael Joyce Loughconera | Bridget Joyce formerly O'Brien | Farmer | Thomas his X O'Brien Present at birth Loughconera | Thirtieth June 1878 | A.B. Heaney |

**20 May 1878 baptismal record of Mary Joyce's brother, John Joyce**

| Name: | John Joyce | Date of Birth: | |
| | | Date of Baptism: | 20-May-1878 |
| Address: | Loughconniera | Parish/District: | CARNA |
| Gender: | Male | County | Co. Galway |
| | | Denomination: | Roman Catholic |
| Father: | Michael Joyce | Mother: | Bridget O'Brien |
| Occupation: | | | |
| Sponsor 1 / Informant 1: | John O'Brien | Sponsor 2 / Informant 2: | Barbara O'Brien |

**11 February 1932 civil death record of Mary Joyce's brother, John Joyce**

| 38 | 1932 Eleventh February Loughconeera Clifden R.D. | John Joyce | M. | Married | 54 years | Farmer | T.B. Emphysema 8 years Cardiac Failure Certified | Joseph his X Joyce married Cousin Present at Death Loughconeera | Seventh March 1932 | C.S. O'Connor Registrar. |

**Mary (Joyce) Kelly's sister Sarah (Joyce) Halloran, and her brother John Joyce (dates unknown)**

**7 May 1882 civil birth record of Mary Joyce's sister, Sarah Joyce**

| 207 | 1882 Seventh May Loughconera | Sarah | 7 | Michael Joyce Loughconera | Bridget Joyce formerly O'Brien | Farmer | Barbaia her X O'Brien Present at birth Loughconera | Eighth June 1882 | A.B. Heaney Registrar. |

# Appendix Two

## Verification of my Joyce/O'Brien Family Tree with
## David G. Riley's "Descendants of Patrick O'Brien"

For decades, David Riley researched his family's Irish ancestors, including our 3x great-grandfather, Patrick O'Brien, born about 1790. Riley did not publish his findings but provided printed copies of undated, heavily annotated family trees (but not relevant records) to his relatives. Through DNA testing, I discovered Jim Joyce, a second cousin to both Riley and me, who has a copy of Riley's 200+ page research findings on Patrick O'Brien and generously lent them to me.

I compared Riley's family trees with my Joyce/O'Brien family tree on page 13 of this essay. In the few instances where our trees differed, such as for Mary Joyce, records that were not available to Riley show that my version is correct. The notes accompanying Riley's trees are amazing. They summarize decades of pre-computerized genealogical research that Riley conducted throughout Ireland and the United States, where he interviewed dozens of relatives. He also searched archives in Dublin, County Galway, Salt Lake City, Washington DC and elsewhere. Riley died in 2019.

This Appendix has three parts, each with a snippet from my abbreviated Joyce/O'Brien family tree on page 13, followed by nearly three dozen relevant notes from Riley's compilation of 1,000 notes, using his numbering system from 1 to 1,000. These notes document the family trees he built for descendants of Patrick O'Brien. Riley's notes also independently verify many entries in my Joyce/O'Brien tree because, in nearly every instance, his sources differ from mine. Riley's and my findings about my grandmother Mary Joyce differ substantially due to differences in our sources. I had access to U.S. data sources that were not available to Riley. See page 38.

### Part One–3x and 2x Great-grandparents

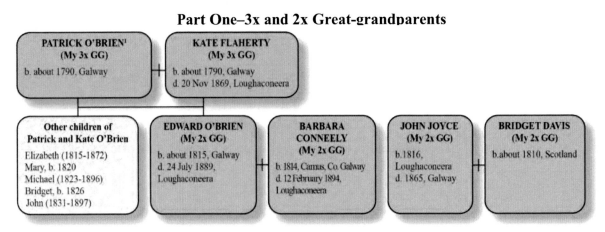

1.    Patrick O'BRIEN - The original information about this ancestor was provided by his great-great-granddaughter Mary (O'Brien) Kilbane of County Galway, Ireland in an undated 1994 letter. Nothing else is known about him. The estimated 1790 year of birth was based only on the estimated birth year of his son Eduirt O'Brien (c 1815-1889) who died in July 1889 at age 74 [see note #197 below]. Patrick is the grandfather of Sean O'Brien (1851-1934).

2.    Kate FLAHERTY (O'BRIEN) - The original information about this ancestor was provided by her great-great-granddaughter Mary (O 'Brien) Kilbane of County Galway in an undated 1994 letter. Nothing else is known about her. She is the wife of Patrick O'Brien [see note #1 above] and her year of birth was arbitrarily estimated to be the same as her husband. Kate is the grandmother of Sean O'Brien (1851-1934).

39.    Bridget O'BRIEN / John Folan - The big question is: Just how many O'Brien families were living in Loughaconeera in the mid-19th century? There couldn't have been too many. My suspicion, and that is all it is, is that this Bridget O'Brien is a sister of Eduirt O'Brien (c 1815-1889) and an aunt of Sean O'Brien (1851-1934). This April 1858 marriage was located in the Carna parish records during an October 2001 research visit to the Family History Library in Salt Lake City, UT. Regrettably, parish marriage records do not record father's names and Irish civil marriage registrations - which do require father's names - did not begin until 1 January 1864. During a visit to County Galway in April/May 2005, information was received from Barbara (Coyne) Naughton of Loughaconeera that the surviving children of this couple had emigrated to England. Barbara provided a copy of a 1994 letter that one of their descendants wrote to the Parish Priest in Carna in an attempt to identify O'Brien cousins. This researcher has been in e-mail contact with the author of that letter - a Brian Foley of England - but no further family details have been uncovered.

7.    Barbara CONNEELY (O'BRIEN) - Initial information about this ancestor was provided by her great-granddaughter Mary (O'Brien) Kilbane of County Galway, Ireland in an undated 1994 letter. The estimated birth year of 1814 is based on her recorded age of 80 at her February 1894 death in Loughaconeera [see note #229 below]. She is the wife of Edward O'Brien (c1815-1889) and the mother of Sean O'Brien (1851-1934).

8.    Edward O'BRIEN - His 1815 estimated year of birth is based on his July 1889 death in Loughaconeera at age 74 [see note #197 below]. Other than his death, the only other known possible reference to Edward in the records is his appearance as a Carna parish baptismal sponsor to Mary Hanrahan in August 1862. He is the father of Sean O'Brien (1851-1934).

## Part Two–O'Brien Great-grandmother and Her Siblings

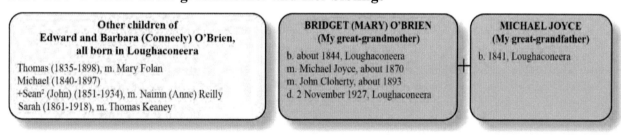

| Other children of Edward and Barbara (Conneely) O'Brien, all born in Loughaconeera | BRIDGET (MARY) O'BRIEN (My great-grandmother) | MICHAEL JOYCE (My great-grandfather) |
|---|---|---|
| Thomas (1835-1898), m. Mary Folan<br>Michael (1840-1897)<br>+Sean[2] (John) (1851-1934), m. Naimn (Anne) Reilly<br>Sarah (1861-1918), m. Thomas Keaney | b. about 1844, Loughaconeera<br>m. Michael Joyce, about 1870<br>m. John Cloherty, about 1893<br>d. 2 November 1927, Loughaconeera | b. 1841, Loughaconeera |

15.    Thomas O'BRIEN - This 1835 estimated year of birth is just that - an estimate. The only basis is the birth of his first child in December 1859. While the relationship has not been positively established in the records, he is believed to be an older brother of Sean O'Brien (1851-1934). Patrick Reilly of County Meath, Ireland believes that Thomas may be an uncle, rather than a brother, of Sean O'Brien - an element of family lore passed down from his father Michael. Thomas falls roughly midway between the c 1815 birth date of Edward O'Brien and the c 1851 birth date of Edward's son Sean, so from this information one could define Thomas either as a younger brother of Edward or an older brother of Sean. I have, for the moment - and based on nothing more than a gut feeling - recorded him as an older brother in this family record.

16.    Mary Folan (O'BRIEN) - The 1839 estimated year of birth is based on her age of 62 as recorded on the 1901 Census of Ireland - a copy of which was provided for her family by the Galway Family History Society West in a report dated 17 July 2001. The census shows the widowed 62-year-old Mary living with her unmarried 35 year old son John O'Brien (1866—1931) in Loughaconeera. However, the record of her March 1931 death in Loughaconeera [see note #682 below] shows her age to be 100 - which computes to a birth year of 1831. Experience has found that the oldest document is usually the most accurate. For that reason, her age of 62 on the 1901 census is assumed to be more accurate and 1839 has been recorded herein for her year of birth. She is the wife of Thomas O'Brien (c1835-1898) and sister-in-law of Sean O'Brien, (1851-1934).

42.    Thomas O'BRIEN / Mary Folan - Details of their January 1859 marriage were located in the Carna parish records by the Galway Family History Society West and provided in a report dated 17 July 2001. The report mentions a note on the parish record indicating the marriage could have taken place in 1858. In that their first known child was born in December 1859 [see note #46 below], it is more likely the marriage took place in 1859.

---

**Summary of Riley's notes on spouses and children of 3 of 7 children of Thomas O'Brien (1835-1898) and Mary Folan (1839-1931).** These surnames appear in the trees of my DNA cousins in Appendix Four, page 46.

1.    Their son Michael O'Brien (1861-1937) had a son, Thomas, baptized 1899, and a daughter, Mary (1887-1917), who married Martin Conneely (1871-1949), later spelled Connolly;

2.    their son Martin (1869-1940) married Nora Flaherty (b. 1874). Among their children were Martin b. 1899 and Mary b. 1902 who married Hugh Walsh (1892-1983); and

3.    their daughter Bridget (1875-c1956) married Dudley Grealish (1861-1935). Grealish's first wife was Nora Halloran. Bridget's son Patrick was baptized in 1901 in Loughaconeera and her daughter Ellen (b. 1911) married Michael Joyce, a grandson of Bridget O'Brien Joyce, and Ellen's second cousin.

---

100.    Sean O'BRIEN/Anne REILLY - Information about their January 1877 marriage was located in both the Carna parish records and Irish civil marriage registers by the Galway Family History Society West and provided in a report dated 28 May 1998. The witness Thomas Sullivan, originally thought to be the father of Anne Sullivan (1903-1996) who married their son Peter O'Brien (1899-1976) in December 1921, is now believed to be the 'other' Thomas Sullivan of Derryrush - a distant cousin on the Reilly side of the family. The other witness, Sarah O'Brien, is Sean's sister. A copy of the marriage register entry was obtained on 17 June 2002.

25.    Sean O'BRIEN - His 1851 estimated year of birth is based on his January 1934 death in Loughaconeera at age 82 [see note #707 below]. It also assumes he would have turned 83 later in 1934. In that he was born before the commencement of church records in the Carna parish, neither his birth nor baptismal dates will ever be known. He is the husband of Anne (Reilly) O'Brien (1853-1925).

26.    Nainin (Anne) REILLY (O 'BRIEN) - Information about her September 1835 baptism was located in the Rosmuc parish records by the Galway Family History Society West and provided in a report dated 28 May 1998. She is the wife of Sean O'Brien (1851-1934).

> **Summary of Riley's notes on the spouses of five of nine children of Sean O'Brien and Anne Reilly.**
>
> 1. Their daughter Barbara (1878-1937) married Joseph Davin (b. 1876);
>
> 2. their daughter Mary (1879-c1952) married Martin Halloran, son of Dennis and Bridget Halloran. One of Mary and Martin's children was Coleman Halloran (1907-1959);
>
> 3. their son John (1883-1953) married Mary Finnerty (b. 1877); and
>
> 4. their son Michael (1884-1949) married Mary Joyce (1889-1963). Their granddaughter is Mary (O'Brien) Burkhead.

22.    Bridget O'BRIEN (Joyce) (Cloherty) - Her estimated 1847 year of birth is based on her November 1927 death record which records her age at death as 80. This death register entry was obtained 6 May 2005, from Jackie McDonagh of Kilkieran who was conducting parish research pursuant to a forthcoming book on the Kilkieran Cemetery and the individuals buried therein. This death register entry provided the very first indication of her year of birth and makes her older than her brother Sean. Earlier estimates showed her to be a younger sister. She is the wife of both Michael Joyce and John Cloherty (c 1841-1930) -both of whom very little is known, and a sister of Sean O'Brien (1851-1934).

162.    Thomas Keaney - Information about his 1883 arrival in the United States was located 28 June 2003 and is recorded on the 1930 US Federal Census for Minnesota where he is shown living with his 2nd wife Mary (Galvin) in Grant township. The lead to this census data was provided by his great-granddaughter Charmaine (Swansen) Boswell of Lombard, IL following establishment of contact with the family on 27 June 2003. Thomas is the husband of Sarah (O'Brien) Keaney (1857-1918) and brother-in-law of Sean O'Brien (1851-1934).

37.    Sarah (O'BRIEN) Keaney- Details of her May 1857 baptism were provided in a Galway Family History Society West Report dated 28 May 1998. The baptismal record shows the name to be Sally, but later records show her name to be Sarah and that is the name used throughout this family record. Her Conneely Godparents are probably her mother Barbara Conneely's brother and his wife. The GFHSW report of May 1998, plus a second report dated 17 July 2001, show her year of birth to be 1859, but I have personally viewed her baptismal record and I am convinced the year is 1857. She is the wife of Thomas Keaney (1859-1943) and the younger sister of Sean O'Brien (1851-1934).

163.    Sarah O'BRIEN / Thomas Keaney - Information about this January 1884 marriage in Chicago was located 3 June 2003 in the on-line Illinois 1763-1900 statewide marriage index. Significant clues leading to this marriage record were the Ellis Island arrivals of her two nieces: Sarah Joyce in July 1900 where reference was made in the ship manifest to her aunt Mrs. Meaney {sic}, and Bridget Joyce in June 1904 where reference was made to her aunt Mrs. Thomas Keaney in Chicago. It was thought these references were to an as yet unknown sibling of Sean O'Brien but locating Sarah after years of research was an enjoyable discovery. Thomas Keaney was the name initially entered as the husband in the Illinois marriage index. There was only one entry, and his wife was Sarah O'Brien. My first thought was: Bingo!!! Initial looks at the 1920 and 1930 US Federal Census records failed to locate their family, but with the help of Sarah's great-granddaughter Charmaine (Swansen) Boswell of Chicago it was determined that Sarah died in 1918 during the Flu Epidemic. Sarah is the younger sister of Sean O'Brien (1851-1934).

94.     Michael JOYCE - Information about his August 1876 birth in Kilkieran was located in the Irish civil birth registers during an October 2001 research visit to the Family History Library in Salt Lake City, UT. Other than his April 1909 arrival in Boston enroute Chicago, IL, very little is known about Michael. He is the son of Bridget (O'Brien) Joyce (c. 847-1927) and nephew of Sean O'Brien (1851-1934).

95.     Michael JOYCE - Details of his September 1876 baptism were located in the Carna parish records by the Galway Family History Society West and provided in a report dated 17 July 2001. The Godfather John (Sean) O'Brien (1851-1934) is the brother of his mother Bridget (O'Brien) Joyce (c1847-1927). It is possible that the Godmother Barbara Conneely is Michael's maternal grandmother.

19.     John CLOHERTY - Information about his estimated 1841 year of birth was located in his Irish civil death register entry which was obtained 6 May 2005 from Jackie McDonagh of Kilkieran who was conducting parish research pursuant to a forthcoming book on the Kilkieran Cemetery and the individuals buried therein. The discovery of this death record, which included his age of 89, was the very first piece of solid information uncovered about this individual. It is strongly suspected that he was a widower when he married the widow Bridget (O'Brien) Joyce (c 1847-1927) - the sister of Sean O'Brien (c 1851-1934). It is also considered a near certainty that his 1st wife was Catherine (KELLY) Cloherty (c 1849-1889) - an aunt of Thomas Sullivan's 2nd wife Barbara (Kelly) Sullivan (1872-1951). The question of whether this John is any relation to Mark Cloherty (cl 838-1928) of Loughaconeera, the father-in-law of Thomas Sullivan's daughter Delia (Sullivan) Cloherty (1901-2000), will remain a matter of future research.

**Part Three: Grandmother Mary (Joyce) Kelly and Her Siblings**

| **MARY A. JOYCE**<br>**(My paternal grandmother)**<br><br>b. 17 November 1872/73,<br>Loughaconeera,<br>emigrated 1888 Source: C<br>m. 1893 Source: C<br>d. 28 July 1918, Oakland, CA | **Other children of Michael and Bridget**<br>**Joyce, all born in Loughaconeera**<br><br>Michael, b. 1876<br>+John Joseph (1878, d. 1932, Loughaconeera)<br>  m. Bridget Conneely (1882-1958)<br>+Sarah (1882, d. 1942, Chicago)<br>  m. Patrick Halloran (1874-1918)<br>Patrick, b. 1883<br>+Bridget⁴ (1886, d. 1952, Chicago)<br>  m. John Coyne (1882-1930)<br>+Margaret (1889, d. 1961, Chicago)<br>  m. Martin Conroy (1885-1959) |
|---|---|

**Note from Joyce Kelly:**
Riley's and my findings about my grandmother Mary Joyce differ substantially due to differences in our sources. I had access to U.S. data sources that were not available to Riley. For example, Mary did not appear in the 1901 Census of Ireland because she had emigrated to America in 1888, according to American immigration and U.S. Federal Census records. Later, she married my grandfather, Michael Kelly, and had six children including my father, Joseph L. Kelly.

77.     Mary JOYCE - Information about her November 1872 birth in Loughaconeera was located in the Irish civil birth registers during an October 2001 research visit to the Family History Library in Salt Lake City, UT. She did not survive to adulthood as evidenced by a second Mary being born to this family in March 1887 (see note #185 below]. Mary is the daughter of Bridget (O'Brien) Joyce and niece of Sean O'Brien.

186.    Mary JOYCE - Details of her March 1887 baptism were located in the Carna parish records during an October 2000 research visit to the Family History Library in Salt Lake City, UT. The information was confirmed by a Galway Family History Society West (GFHSW) report dated 17 July 2001. Her Godfather Martin O'Brien is believed to be her older cousin. In that Mary is not listed with the family on the 1901 Census of Ireland - also provided by the July 2001 GFHSW report, it is possible she died very young. Research will continue. Mary is the daughter of Bridget (O'Brien) Joyce (c 1847-1927) and the niece of Sean O'Brien (1851-1934).

301.    John Joseph JOYCE - Information about his June 1902 arrival in the United States at age 24 in the port of New York was located 2 June 2003 in the on-line Ellis Island arrivals database. Traveling with him on the SS LUCANIA were his Carna parish cousins John O 'Brien (age 19) and Bridget Connolly (age 20) who were all traveling to Chicago. Bridget is believed to be the same Bridget Conneely who later married John in Chicago. John and his wife Bridget later returned to Loughaconeera after their first child John was born in Chicago in July 1904. John is the son of Bridget (O'Brien) (Joyce) Cloherty (c 1847-1927) and nephew of Sean O'Brien (1851-1934).

303.    Bridget CONNEELY - Information about Bridget's June 1902 arrival in the United States at age 20 in the port.of New York, was located 2 June 2003 in the on-line Ellis Island arrivals database. Traveling with her on the SS LUCANIA were her Carna parish cousins John O'Brien (age 19) and John Joyce (age24) who were all traveling to Chicago. Bridget is believed to be the same Bridget Conneely who later married John Joyce in Chicago. The 'cousin' relationship was indicated on the ship manifest where it states that Bridget would be joining her 'cousin' Sarah Joyce at 121 Ontario St. in Chicago. Sarah is the sister of Bridget's travel partner John Joyce, but the cousin relationship of Bridget Conneely to Sarah and John Joyce is not understood. The relationship may derive from the fact that the O'Brien grandmother of the two Joyce siblings was Barbara (Conneely) O'Brien. If Bridget is the wife of John Joyce [research will continue on this point], she and John later returned to Loughaconeera after their first child John was born in Chicago in July 1904.

283.    Sarah JOYCE - Information about her July 1900 arrival in the United States at age 18 in the port of New York was located in the on-line Ellis Island database. The ship manifest does not conclusively prove she is of the correct family, but the address of Kilkerrin and the age of 18 matches precisely other known family information. For these reasons, a temporary assumption is being made that she is family. Traveling with her on the SS CAMPANIA were her Kilkerrin neighbors Mary Grealish (age 25) whose final destination was recorded as New York, and Annie Coyne (age 20) who was traveling to Chicago. Sarah, whose final destination was the home of an aunt "Mrs. Meany" then living at 13 E. Superior St. in Chicago, is believed to be the daughter of Bridget (O'Brien) (Joyce) Cloherty (c 1847-1927) and niece of Sean O'Brien (1851-1934). On 3 June 2003, all doubt about the identity of this Sarah and her aunt Mrs. 'Meany' was clarified when the January 1884 marriage of Thomas Keaney to Sarah O'Brien was located online in the Illinois statewide marriage index (see note #163 above]. Sarah Joyce is indeed the daughter of Bridget (O'Brien) Joyce and her aunt is her mother's sister.

146.    Sarah (JOYCE) Halloran – Information about her May 1882 birth in Loughaconeera was located in the Irish civil birth registers by Galway Family History Society West and provided in a report dated 17 July 2001. Very little is known about Sarah, but she did emigrate to Chicago, IL in July 1900 [see note #283 below]. On 21 March 20024 in an e-mail received from Diana Coyne of Chicago (another Galway researcher), mention is made of the May 1904 marriage in Chicago of Diana's cousin Patrick Halloran to a

Sarah Joyce. Diana is related to the two Finnerty sisters (Mary and Catherine) who married Sean O'Briens' sons John and Martin in Chicago. The mother of the Finnerty sisters was Barbara Coyne – thus the connection to Diana. On 11 July 2004, Sarah's August 1942 obituary was received from an on-line contributor, and the recorded sisters Bridget and Margaret matched perfectly with the children on Bridget (O'Brien) Joyce. On 12 July 2004, yet another on-line contributor provided Sarah's sister Bridget's September 1952 obituary, and the recorded siblings prove conclusively that both Sarah and Bridget are daughters of Bridget O'Brien.

406.　Patrick JOYCE - Initial information about Patrick's death was received 30 December 2005 via an e-mail from his grandnephew Tim Coyne of Chicago. The e-mail included burial details for Patrick at Mount Carmel Cemetery in Hillside, IL just outside of Chicago. The grave owner was recorded as Bridget Joyce - believed to be Patrick's sister. A call to the cemetery - also on 30 December - provided information about the death of James Martin Coyne (1942-1944), Bridget (Joyce) Coyne's grandson. Details of his death were confirmed 26 January 2006 with receipt of his city of Chicago death certificate. Patrick is the son of Bridget (O'Brien) Joyce (c 1847-1927) and nephew of Sean O'Brien.

182.　Bridget (JOYCE) Coyne – Apparently, there are no extant birth or baptismal records available for this daughter of Bridget (O'Brien) Joyce (c 1856-1927). Her 1886 estimated year of birth is based on her age and position in the family as recorded on the 1901 Census of Ireland provided by the Galway Family History Society West in a report dated 17 July 2001. On 21 March 2004 in an e-mail received from Diana Coyne of Chicago (another Galway researcher), mention was made of the May 1904 marriage in Chicago of Diana's cousin Patrick Halloran to a Sarah Joyce. As background, Diana is also related to the two Finnerty sisters (Mary and Catherine) who married Sean O'Brien's sons John and Martin in Chicago. Patrick Halloran's wife Sarah then became the object of intense research, and efforts to prove that Sarah and Bridget were sisters proved successful in July 2004. On 11 July 2004, Sarah's August 1942 newspaper obituary was received from an on-line contributor, and the recorded sisters Bridget and Margaret match perfectly with Sarah's family. On 12 July 2004, yet another on-line contributor provided Bridget's September 1952 obituary, and the recorded siblings prove conclusively that both Sarah and Bridget are daughters of Bridget O'Brien. Details of Bridget's family were then located in Chicago, IL on the 1930 US Federal Census. Bridget is the wife of John Coyne (c 1882-1930) of Connemara and niece of Sean O'Brien (1851-1934). An e-mail received 28 August 2006 from Mary K. Grant of Chicago, a granddaughter of Bridget, provided the 15 August 1886 birth date.

191.　Margaret (Joyce) CONROY - There are, apparently, no extant birth or baptismal records available for this daughter of Bridget (O'Brien) Joyce (c 1847-1927). Her 1888 estimated year of birth is based on her age and position in the family as recorded on the 1901 Census of Ireland provided by the Galway Family History Society West in a report dated 17 July 2001. Through a series of discoveries associated with her siblings, telephone contact with Margaret's son Lawrence in Evanston, IL was made on 20 July 2004, and a specific birth date for Margaret of 02 February 1888 was provided. Margaret is the wife of Martin Conroy (c 1886-1959) and niece of Sean O ' Brien (1851-1934).

358.　Margaret (Joyce) CONROY • Margaret's June 1907 arrival in the US was located I l January 2006 in the on-line Boston passenger arrivals. She arrived on board SS SAXONIA enroute to Chicago, IL to join her sister Bridget Joyce then living at 75 East Huron Street. Traveling with Maggie (that was the name on the manifest) were Bridget Flaherty and Bridget Coyne - both of whom were also traveling to Chicago, and both of whom (along with Maggie) show Kilkieran as their last residence in Ireland. Margaret is the wife of Martin Conroy (c 1886-1959), daughter of Bridget (O'Brien) Joyce (c 1847-1927) and niece of Sean O'Brien (1851-1934).

350.   Martin CONROY - Details of his May 1906 arrival. in New York were located 29 January 2005 in the on-line Ellis Island arrivals database. It will require additional evidence to prove that this Martin is the husband of Margaret Joyce, but the evidence points very strongly in that direction. Martin was traveling with his cousin John Halloran, and the passage was paid by John's brother Patrick Halloran who was then living at 75 East Huron Street in Chicago. It should be noted that Sarah (O'Brien) Keaney (1857-1918) - the aunt of Martin's future wife Margaret - was living.at 52 East Huron Street in 1898. John's brother Patrick is believed to be the husband of Sarah (Joyce) Halloran (1882-1942). Larry Conroy of Evanston, IL- Martin's son - confirmed via an e-mail on 06 April 2007 that this passenger arrival is that of his father. Martin is the husband of Margaret (Joyce) Conroy (1888-1961), son-in-law of Bridget (O'Brien) Joyce (c 1847-1927) and nephew (by marriage) of Sean O'Brien (1851-1934).

# Appendix Three

## Halloran Family History

Peggy Calhoun provided a brief history of the Halloran family (excerpted here), written by Joseph Halloran in 1977. Joseph was a son of Patrick (1871-1918) and Sarah (Joyce) Halloran (1883-1942) and uncle of Dan Halloran. Sarah was a sister of our grandmother, Mary Joyce.

Joseph Halloran's essay includes (1) brief descriptions of their lives in Ireland and in an Irish neighborhood of Chicago, where Mary Joyce's three sisters and their Aunt Sarah lived (our grandmother Mary had already settled in Oakland, California); (2) a list of names of some of the children and grandchildren of Mary's sisters; and (3) a brief description of Ireland from a *Life* magazine article. Parts (2) and (3) are not reproduced here.

### Beginning of the Halloran Family History, written by Joseph Halloran in 1977

```
This history of the Halloran Family was composed by Joe Halloran
in Pinellas Park, Florida, in 1977.  Information about our family
in Ireland was supplied by our aunt, Julia Halloran Masterson,
now age eighty nine.  Also by Sarah Halloran Casey and her sister,
Ann Halloran Masterson, who along with their sister, Nora Masterson,
were born in Ireland and came to America beginning in 1948.

The house pictures were taken in 1968 by a cousin, Eileen Stevens,
and by Aunt Julia and Rita Jacobsen.  They are of the Halloran
family home located in Rosmuck, County Galway.  The house over-
looks an inlet of Galway Bay and at high tide the water covers
some of their land.  The Connemara Mountains, called The Twelve
Bens, are in the background.  The house had four rooms and a
loft.  It is presently used as a barn.  Ann says one year they
won a flower growing contest put on by the town.

Galway is rocky and mountainous country and is located in Western
Ireland.  The Halloran farm is located two miles from the town of
Rosmuck.  It is two miles from school and three miles to church.
Transportation for the kids of those days, around 1900, was by
walking.  Schooling then only amounted to three or four years.
Aunt Julia says chores to do included walking three miles to
milk the cows and digging out peat bogs for fire fuel.  It was
necessary for the children to move to America since their small
farms could not support all of them and Ireland being an agri-
cultural country there were no industries they could work at.
The oldest of the family would usually emigrate first and then
save enough money for the next one until all or most of the
children came over.  Steerage class on the steamship, which is
the bottom of the boat, and seasickness were common and the
journey took 8 to 10 days.

How hard it must have been to leave home forever knowing you
would not see your parents again and how much harder for the
parents.  My mother said she cried for a whole year.  Aunt
Julia was one of the lucky ones to make the trip back home.
```

**[Two notes from Joyce**: (1) Our great-grandparents, Michael and Bridget (O'Brien) Joyce, had seven children. See the abbreviated family tree on page 13 for the names and birthdates of their seven children; and (2) "Father" (below) was Patrick Halloran (1874-1918) and "Mother" was Sarah (Joyce) Halloran (1882-1942). Sarah was a sister of our grandmother Mary Joyce. The families of Patrick and Sarah likely knew each other in Ireland.]

## Continuation of the Halloran Family History, written by Joseph Halloran in 1977

Father was born in 1874 and died in 1918 at age 44. Mother was
born in 1883 and died in 1942 at age 59. They were married in
Chicago in 1904 and lived at 75 E. Huron Street which is on the
near north side less than a mile from downtown. Three oldest
boys were born John (1904), Pat (1906) and Joe (1908) and
baptized at St. Dominic's Church (all of us were born at home).

Due to our father's health (he had asthma) we moved to Stockton,
California (236 W. Grant St.) in 1911 for two years. This in-
volved traveling coach train with three children aged 3, 5 and 7.
I remember it was rugged traveling. Four or five days and delayed
for a few days due to a storm. Food was bought when the train
stopped. Tom was born there in 1912, one of a set of twins
(the other died at birth).

In 1913 we returned to Chicago. My father worked as a well-digger,
digging foundations for buildings. This work was too difficult
for him so he worked as a laborer at a warehouse (Sibleys).

In those days all immigrants settled in their own nationality
neighborhoods. We lived in the Irish - above the Italians and
below the Germans, who lived north of North Avenue. The Italians
were south of Chicago Avenue.

We lived crudely then compared to now. No packaged or refrigerated
foods. We shopped every day at the neighborhood grocery store.
Ice was delivered - 25 pounds. In winter, food was kept outside
on the windowsill box to prevent spoiling. We had a wood stove
in the kitchen for cooking and a coal stove in the parlor for
heating. Bedrooms were cold. We'd dress by the stove - long
underwear, of course. Sometimes the toilet was in the hall.
Slept three or four to a bed - head to foot. Bath once a week,
usually on Saturday, in a washtub, or shower at the local YMCA.
We lived in houses without electricity, using kerosene lamps
which could be carried where needed. The winters then were
colder and the summers warmer than now.

As our fortunes improved we moved farther north to the Immaculate
Conception Parish (1432 North Park Avenue). Bill was born in
1915. We lived on the northwest corner of Wells and Siegel Streets,
above a saloon. Our father was a very sociable man, unlike our
mother who was quiet. There were quite a few parties at our
house when they would roll up the rugs and do the Irish dances.

Our father died March 28, 1918, from the flu epidemic. We were
living on Orleans Street opposite the I.C. Church. His wake was
held at home for two nights. The men would gather in the kitchen,
drink an occasional whiskey, smoke clay pipes and talk. The women
sat in the parlor (front room) where the open casket was displayed,

keening or wailing loudly as was the old country custom, and
consoling the widow and children. After the Mass, the body
was transported by Train to Mt. Carmel Cemetery. Our ages
were: John 13, Pat 12, Joe 10, Tom 6, and Bill 2.

Even with the help of our aunts and uncles our mother had to go
to work. We had always lived near our mother's sisters - the
Coynes and the Conroys - and our father's sister - the Morans
(Rita Jacobsen). The Coynes lived downstairs and took care of
the kids. Our mother worked in the convent laundry. She also
swept the school rooms every day with our help. We swept under
the desks and the stairways. We also delivered papers. Each
younger one inheriting the job when the older ones went to full
time work. John and Pat worked for Sprague Warner Mail Order
House as messenger boys on roller skates in the summer. When
they graduated from grammar school at age 14 they worked full
time and went to continuation school, learning shorthand and
typing, until they were 16. Later they both worked for the
railroads. After grammar school, Joe went to Quigley for five
years and one year to Mundelein. Discipline was strict and
studies were hard and I didn't have the fortitude for that
career. I guess I too was a party boy like my father. So were
Tom and Bill, but John and Pat were the quiet type like our
mother - except Pat had the redhead's temper. Tom went to
St. Patrick's High School for two years. Then the depression
started in 1929. Pat married in 1931, John in 1933. The
depression was rough, except that after walking downtown to
look for a job every morning, we had the rest of the day off.
We were near Lake Michigan for swimming in the summer time and
near Lincoln Park for skating in winter. Our parish had a
boy's club and girl's club with clubrooms and a big hall for
athletics, theater, bingo and dancing. We didn't need much
money to have our fun.

Joe, Tom and Bill were living together with our mother. We
never had to go on relief but no two of us could get jobs at
the same time so we lived on about $15.00 a week. In 1933 and
the summer of 1934 Joe worked as a roller chair tour guide at
the World's Fair which was held outside of Soldier's Field and
ran from 12th Street to 39th Street. Shick Coyne worked there
in 1934. (Dick Perrin and Martin Nee worked there also at
Pabst Casino Restaurant where Ben Bernie's band played.) It was
an exciting place to work. Bill graduated from St. Michael's
High School in 1934. Tom worked for States Hand Laundry across
from Holy Name Cathedral. Bill got a good job with Dupont
Chemical Company. I worked for American Steel Foundries in
the Wrigley Building for a few years. Bill and Joe helped Tom
in the laundry business which we bought and Tom operated (Ann
Eich also worked with us). I worked for Parmalee Transportation
Company as an agent. They transferred passengers and baggage
between the railroad stations and hotels. (Schick Coyne also
worked for them.) Tom worked for them as a passenger car driver
on a split shift, morning and evening basis, and worked the
laundry in between. Our mother worked as a chambermaid at the

Ambassador Hotel until she was in her fifties. You couldn't make
her quit - she liked it. We sold the laundry business - we found
out you're not your own boss - all your customers are. Tom got
a job as electrician for Western Electric Company. He got married
in 19  . In 1939 the war started in Europe. In 1941 Pearl Harbor
was attacked and Bill was drafted. I was deferred as sole support
of our mother. We lived on Eugene Street near Wells. Our mother
died in 1942 at age 59 from bronchitis. Bill's being drafted
hurt a lot. The morning Bill left was the first time I heard
her swear. She called Hitler an S.O.B. She was a wonderful
person as everyone who knew her knows. All the kids called her
"Aunt Sarah." She had a great sense of humor. We'd say "you're
coughing better today, Ma." She'd answer "I was practicing all
night." She is also buried at Mt. Carmel near our father's grave.
After her death I went into service. So did Tom and Pat. John
being older was exempt. Bill married while in service in 19  .
Joe married in 1948.

Bill became a Captain as head of supply at a station hospital on
Espiritu Santo Island in the New Hebrides Islands in the Pacific.
Tom was in the CBs as an electrician and was stationed on the
Island of Guam in the Pacific. Joe was Staff Sergeant in the
anti-aircraft and was in all the battles in Europe (except Italy)
with the 2nd Infantry Division. Pat was a PFC ammo-bearer in a
machine gun company for the 104th Infantry Division and experienced
the closest contact with the enemy. Well, that's the way he was.

As for our work. Bill was an office manager for Dupont Chemical
Company. Nancy works in a bank at Libertyville. Tom was an
electrician at Western Electric. Eileen is a school teacher with
a Master's Degree (our best educated family member). Joe and
Junice were inventory managers for the Navy at Great Lakes.
Pat worked as supervisor for freight forwarding for the Chesapeake
and Ohio Railroad. Bernie was a saleslady at Weiboldt's. John
was supervisor in billing for the Burlington Railroad. Mary
worked for the Bell Telephone Company.

That ends the story of our lives as a family. I wouldn't trade
it for anyone else's - and I hope each family continues its own
history as I have tried to do here.

**Sarah (Joyce) and Patrick Halloran and Family in Chicago, date unknown**

# Appendix Four

## A Genealogical Proof Argument for the Loughaconeera Origin of Mary Joyce

Genealogical records indicate that my American Mary Joyce and Peggy Calhoun's Irish Mary Joyce are the same person. However, we cannot demonstrate that they are the same person because Mary Joyce's American records begin with her 1888 immigration when she was nearly 16 years old, while Mary's Irish records end with her birth and baptism in Ireland in 1872.

This appendix addresses this issue by examining the DNA evidence that the American Mary Joyce and the Irish Mary Joyce are the same person. I do this with a Genealogical Proof Argument[36] to identify Most Recent Common Ancestors with: (1) several dozen DNA-matched members of the Rosmuc Area Genealogy and DNA Facebook Group; and (2) five of my strongest DNA matches[37] on FamilyTreeDNA and AncestryDNA. I tried to contact my DNA cousins with the strongest matches to share information. Rosmuc Area FB Group members generally responded, but subscribers to FamilyTreeDNA and AncestryDNA generally did not respond. **Surnames of living people are displayed below only if they consented to being included in this family history.**

### DNA matches with members of the Rosmuc Area Genealogy and DNA Facebook (FB) Group

After I joined the Rosmuc FB Group, Noel Murphy, a Group founder and administrator, ran GEDmatch data with the Matchmaker tool for my brother, sisters, and me. Soon after, Noel contacted me because he thought that my Joyce ancestors might be included in the family tree of Peggy Calhoun, a Rosmuc Group member. Matchmaker identified my DNA matches with 21 members of the Rosmuc Group, including Dan Halloran, with a 442 cM FamilyTreeDNA match.[38]

After I published the names of my DNA matches on the Group FB page, Peggy Calhoun, a cousin on the Halloran side of Dan's family, contacted me because her well-documented Ancestry family tree (page 10 of this family history) includes a possible common family member—my paternal grandmother, Mary Joyce. Peggy's tree shows that her Mary Joyce was born in Loughaconeera in County Galway, which is eight miles by land and four miles by sea from Rosmuc.

---

[36] Terri Stern, founder of My Genealogy Tutor, Terri taught me how to apply the Genealogical Proof Standard (GPS)- a formal process to produce credible, valid findings-in this research. A Genealogical Proof Argument (GPA)-the most rigorous proof option of the GPS-uses DNA test results and genealogical records in an extensive documented narrative to explain the rationale for proving a conclusion. See *Genealogy Standards,* Board for Certification of Genealogists, New York, 2019 and *Mastering Genealogical Proof*, Thomas W. Jones, National Genealogical Society Special Topic Series No. 107, 2013.

[37] I analyzed those five with the most complete and well-documented family trees among my strongest DNA matches.

[38] DNA test results differ across DNA testing companies because they use different methodologies to calculate cMs. FamilyTreeDNA improved their methodology and released new match results in July 2021. They are included here.

**Excerpt from my abbreviated Joyce/O'Brien family tree on page 13**

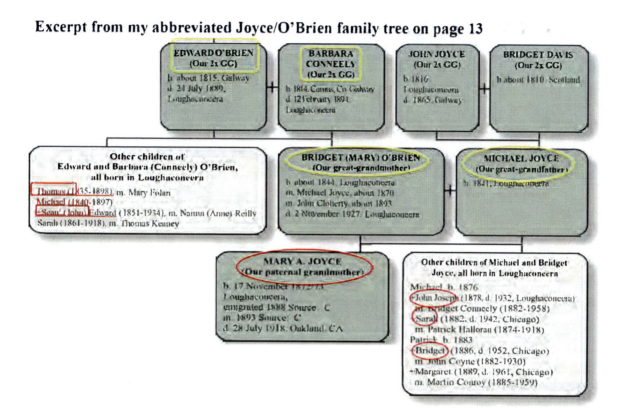

+**Their parents are our Most Recent Common Ancestors (MRCAs)** because I am a confirmed second or third cousin DNA match with one or more of their descendants, according to their and my well-documented family trees. MRCAs are the closest shared ancestors between two DNA-matched individuals.

I reviewed documents attached to Peggy's tree and we jointly concluded that our Mary Joyces likely were the same person. Later, after researching and confirming every entry, I incorporated the Joyce line in Peggy's tree into mine. My full family tree, https://www.ancestry.com/family-tree/tree/160255584?cfpid=282094565936, includes 292 people, 408 records, and 68 images.

The chart above, from my abbreviated Joyce & O'Brien family tree on page 13, displays the surnames of many of my 21 Rosmuc FB Group DNA matches and virtually every surname above occurs in the list of "ancestral surnames"[39] of my 21 matches. Turning to my brother and sisters, the DNA Matchmaker tool identified 44 matches for Jim, 38 matches for Kate, and 32 matches for Julie with other Rosmuc Area FB members (totaling 114 matches in addition to my 21). There are several dozen instances where two or three of us share matches. Among our 135 matches with Rosmuc FB members, between 50-70 are unique descendants of ancestors that one or more of us share with Group members. The remaining 65-85 matches duplicate these unique descendants.

The next section of the Genealogical Proof Argument validates my paternal great-grandparents as our Most Recent Common Ancestors using family trees of three of my strongest DNA matches— Dan Halloran (442 cMs), Kevin X (384 cMs), and James Joyce (361 cMs).

---

[39] During the 19th century and earlier, small rural Irish townlands were kinship villages, where most residents were related by marriage through many generations.

**Validating my paternal great-grandparents as MRCAs with my DNA matches**

The chart on the prior page shows my Joyce line, marked with ovals and my O'Brien line, marked with squares. My paternal great-grandparents, Michael Joyce (b. 1841) and Bridget Mary (O'Brien) Joyce (1844-1927), marked with yellow ovals, were the parents of seven children, including my paternal grandmother, Mary Joyce (1872/73-1918, red oval), my granduncle John Joseph (1878-1932), and grandaunts Bridget (1886-1952) and Sarah Joyce (1882-1942), all with red ovals. My tests on AncestryDNA and FamilyTreeDNA show strong matches with James Joyce, who descends from John; Kevin X, who descends from Bridget; and Dan Halloran, who descends from Sarah. The Joyce line, on family trees below, shows that we are second cousins and our MRCAs are our great-grandparents, Michael Joyce and Bridget Mary (O'Brien) Joyce.

**James Joyce, my 361 cM AncestryDNA match**

Our MRCAs are the parents of James' maternal grandfather, John Joseph Joyce, and my paternal grandmother, Mary (Joyce) Kelly, who were siblings. James' 361 cMs shared with me and 249 cMs shared with my brother Jim support our second cousin relationship. Both of James' parents carried the surname Joyce. James' maternal Joyces came from the Aran Islands.

**The Joyce Line on James Joyce's Family Tree**

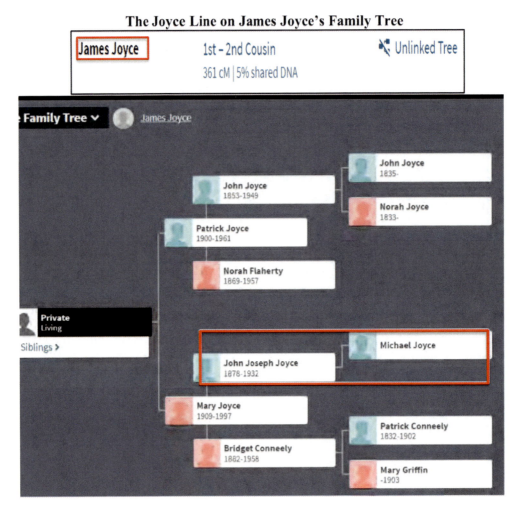

**Kevin X, my 384 cM AncestryDNA match**

Our MRCAs are the parents of Kevin's maternal grandmother, Bridget (Joyce) Coyne (1886-1952), and my paternal grandmother, Mary (Joyce) Kelly (1872/73-1918), who were sisters. Kevin's 384 cMs shared with me and 277 cMs shared with my brother Jim support our second cousin relationship. Kevin's surname is redacted because he did not respond to my emails requesting permission to include his full name.

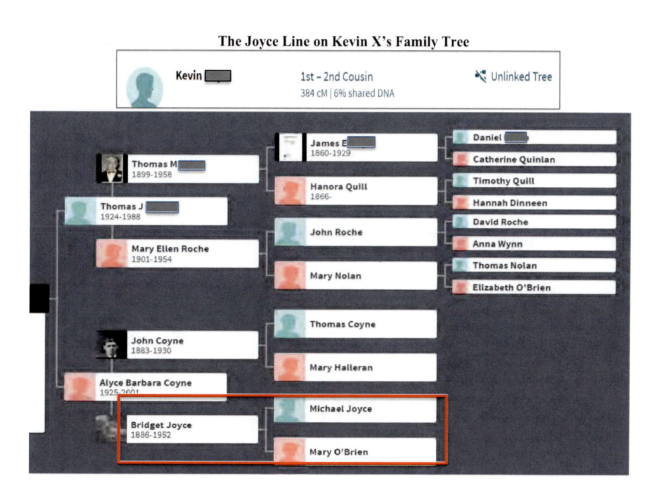

ThruLines on the next page show that five of my DNA matches and I linked our AncestryDNA test results to our Ancestry family trees, facilitating development of AncestryDNA's ThruLines to help identify our MRCAs. (Note that the trees of James Joyce and Kevin X above are "unlinked"). Until DNA matches and family trees are validated, ThruLines are only suggestive. ThruLines suggest that my great-grandparents, Michael Joyce (b.1841) and Bridget Mary (O'Brien) Joyce (1844-1927), are MRCAs of me and five descendants of my grandmother Mary's sisters, Sarah (1882-1942) and Bridget (1886-1952).

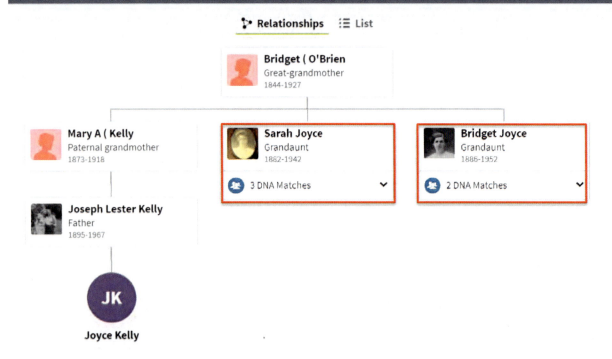

## Dan Halloran, my 442 cM FamilyTreeDNA match

Dan Halloran tested at FamilyTreeDNA, not Ancestry, therefore, he is not included in the ThruLines matches above. Our MRCAs are the parents of Dan's paternal grandmother, Sarah (Joyce) Halloran (1882-1942), and my paternal grandmother, Mary (Joyce) Kelly (1872/73-1918), who were sisters.

Dan transferred his FamilyTreeDNA match results to GEDmatch, facilitating verification by Terri Stern, founder of My Genealogy Tutor, that Dan's DNA shared segments triangulate with other matches descended from Michael Joyce and Bridget O'Brien. Terri confirmed that Dan and I share 17 segments; Dan and my brother Jim share 14 segments; Dan and my sister Julie share 18 segments; and Dan and my sister Kate share 15 segments. **There is a solid genealogical proof argument for our MRCA relationship based on (1) shared DNA segments with Dan; (2) his total cMs shared with me (461), Jim (278), Julie (366) and Kate (305); and (3) my validation of the Joyce line on Dan's tree with genealogical records for every entry.** Dan's tree is displayed on the next page.

### The Joyce Line on Daniel Halloran's Family Tree

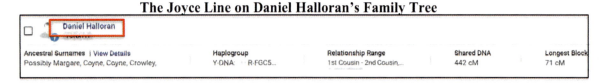

| | | Daniel Halloran | | | | |
|---|---|---|---|---|---|---|
| Ancestral Surnames | View Details | | Haplogroup | Relationship Range | Shared DNA | Longest Block |
| Possibly Margare, Coyne, Coyne, Crowley, | | | Y-DNA: R-FGC5... | 1st Cousin - 2nd Cousin,... | 442 cM | 71 cM |

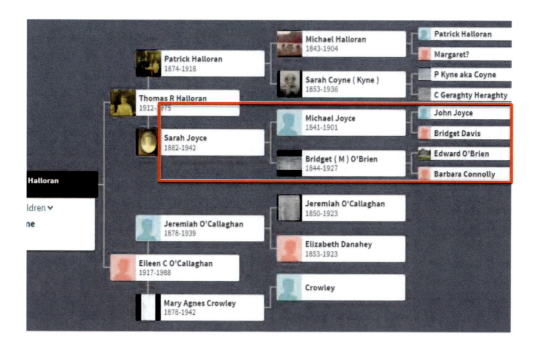

## Validating my paternal 2x great-grandparents as MRCAs with my DNA Matches

The chart on page 47 shows that my O'Brien line begins with my 2x great-grandparents, Edward O'Brien (abt. 1815-1889) and Barbara Conneely (1814-1894), marked with yellow squares, who were the parents of five children, including my paternal great-grandmother, Bridget Mary (O'Brien) Joyce (yellow oval), and my great-granduncles Thomas (1835-1898) and Sean (John Edward) O'Brien (1851-1934), marked with red squares. I match on AncestryDNA with eleven descendants of my great-granduncles–Thomas and Sean–who linked their AncestryDNA test results to their Ancestry family trees facilitating AncestryDNA's ThruLines analyses, below.

### ThruLines showing potential relationships between my DNA matches and our MRCAs

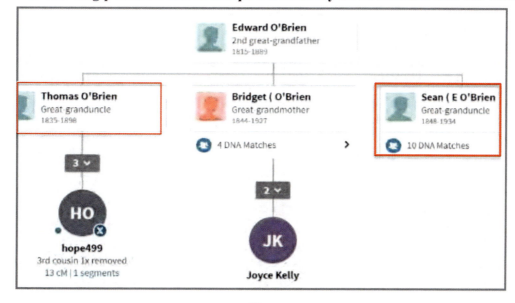

ThruLines display my paternal 2x great-grandparents, Edward O'Brien and Barbara Conneely, as possible MRCAs of me and eleven AncestryDNA matched descendants of Thomas and Sean. I tried to contact each Ancestry cousin but none responded. Therefore, I turned to my FTDNA matches with Paraic McDonagh, a 99 cM match at FamilyTreeDNA, who responded to my inquiry; and Hugh Walsh, a 136cM FTDNA match, who is deceased, but has a helpful family tree.

According to Terri Stern, the Genealogical Proof Statement to validate Edward and Barbara as MRCAs of Paraic, Hugh and me requires a triangulated match across a segment shared by three different descendants of our MRCAs. My siblings and I descend from Bridget. My third cousin Paraic McDonogh descends from Bridget's brother Sean, and my third cousin Hugh Walsh descends from Thomas, a brother of Bridget and Sean.

> Terri conducted the following DNA segment analyses at FamilyTreeDNA to meet the genealogical proof standard for DNA confirmation of a 2x great-grandparent:
>
> On Chromosome 9, Paraic, Hugh and I triangulate on a segment from 128 to 136.4.
>
> On Chromosome 5, Paraic, Hugh, my brother Jim and I triangulate on a segment from 164.9 to 172.

This section of the Genealogical Proof Statement concludes with the O'Brien line in the family trees of Paraic McDonogh and Hugh Walsh, showing how they descend from our MRCAs, our 2 x great-grandparents, Edward O'Brien (abt. 1815-1889) and Barbara Coneelly (1814-1894). Our MRCAs are the parents of Thomas, Sean and my great-grandmother, Bridget Mary (O'Brien) Joyce. The O'Brien line on Hugh's and Paraic's family trees are displayed below.

### The O'Brien Line on the Family Tree of Hugh Walsh, my 136 cM FTDNA match

**The O'Brien Line on the Family Tree of Paraic McDonagh, my 99 cM FamilyTreeDNA match**

The table below summarizes results of the Genealogical Proof Statement (GPS) showing my great-grandparents, Michael Joyce and Bridget Mary (O'Brien) Joyce, as the MRCAs of me and three of my strongest DNA matches - James Joyce, Dan Halloran, and Kevin X. The table also displays the names and parents of five additional genetic cousins in the "AncestryDNA Joyce-O'Brien" Group created by Terri Stern – Deidre X, Mary X, Timothy X, Erin X and Daniel X. I did not include these five cousins in my GPS because they do not have trees or their trees do not include a Joyce or O'Brien line. Also, they did not respond to my emails requesting collaboration.

**MRCAs with eight DNA cousin descendants of four of Mary (Joyce) Kelly's six siblings**

| Mary's siblings and their spouses, see Joyce/O'Brien family tree, page 13. | My great-grandparents, Michael Joyce and Bridget Mary (O'Brien) Joyce, through my grandmother Mary (Joyce) Kelly's….. |
|---|---|
| John Joseph (1878–1932) m. Bridget Conneely (1882-1958) | brother John Joyce, grandfather of my 361 cM/ second cousin match with **James Joyce**. |
| Sarah (1882 – 1942) m. Patrick Halloran (1874-1918) | sister Sarah (Joyce) Halloran, grandmother of my 438 cM/second cousin match with **Dan Halloran**. |
| | sister Sarah (Joyce) Halloran, grandmother of my 206 cM/second cousin match with **Deidre X.** |

| Mary's siblings and their spouses, see Joyce/O'Brien family tree, page 13. | My great-grandparents, Michael Joyce and Bridget Mary (O'Brien) Joyce, through my grandmother Mary (Joyce) Kelly's….. |
|---|---|
| Bridget (1886 – 1952 m. John Coyne (1882-1930) | sister Bridget (Joyce) Coyne, grandmother of my 448 cM/second cousin match with **Mary X**.<br><br>sister Bridget (Joyce) Coyne, grandmother of my 387 cM/second cousin match with **Timothy X**.<br><br>sister Bridget (Joyce) Coyne, grandmother of my 384 cM/second cousin match with **Kevin X**. |
| Margaret (1889 – 1961) m. Martin Conroy (1885-1959) | sister Margaret (Joyce) Conroy, grandmother of my 301 cM match with **Erin X**.<br><br>sister Margaret (Joyce) Conroy, grandmother of my 244 cM match with **Daniel X** |

**This concludes my DNA Proof Argument. The evidence overwhelmingly supports the conclusion that our Mary (Joyce) Kelly (1872/73-1918) originated in Loughaconeera, County Galway**. She was one of seven children of Michael Joyce (b. 1841) and Bridget Mary (O'Brien) Joyce (abt.1844-1927) and a MRCA-confirmed granddaughter of Edward O'Brien (abt. 1815-1889) and Barbara Conneely (1814-1894) with more than a dozen 99cM and higher confirmed DNA matches.

# Appendix Five

## Sean O'Briain–introduction, obituary and story, "The King's Son"

Sean O'Briain (John O'Brien in English, 1851-1934) was an uncle of Mary Joyce (see page 13). He lived and died in Loughaconeera, was a farmer-fisherman, and a well-known *sgéalaidhthe*–traditional Gaelic storyteller. Three collectors of Irish folktales published his stories. O'Briain spoke only Irish and was unknown to English-speakers until 1894, when the American folklore collector, Jeremiah Curtin, published an English-language collection of Irish folk tales, *Hero Tales of Ireland* (Macmillan and Co, 1894) with four of O'Briain's stories.[40] Forty years later, Sean Mac Giollarnath, who wrote O'Briain's obituary, published three of O'Briain's folktales in an Irish collection. Seamus O'Duilearga (James Delargy in English, 1899-1980), a founder of The Irish Folklore Society, also collected and preserved stories, including many of O'Briain's.

The 1999 book of essays, *International Folkloristics* (Alan Dundes, ed., Rowman Littlefield, 1999), includes O'Duilearga's essay, "Irish Tales and Story-Tellers." O'Duilearga wrote about a visit to Sean O'Briain's farm: "In the Spring of 1932 I approached the house of the story-teller… I shall never forget, as long as I live, the tale I heard. It was AaTh313[41] and although I have often heard it, I never met anyone who told is so well. O'Briain was the finest storyteller I have ever met–or ever shall meet. He would have been regarded a good storyteller 500 years ago…" (p. 171).

Elsewhere in "Irish Tales and Story-Tellers," O'Duilearga wrote: "The old-time Gaelic story-teller was a conscious literary artist, proud of his art, jealous of his rivals, eager to pass on the tradition as it had come to him, conservative as to form, order and plot; but the style and language are stamped with his own personality. He felt at liberty to elaborate inside the traditional framework of the narrative … and to clothe the commonplaces of fiction with the rich garments of poetic prose…these features of the Gaelic oral tradition link the folk-tale of today to the aristocratic manuscript literature of the eighth century" (p. 161).

**Sean O'Briain (left and right), Loughaconeera, about 1930, and a young storyteller (center)**

---

[40] One of O'Briain's stories appears below and two of his folktales are included in Appendix Seven, page 71.

[41] This class is for "tales of supernatural adversaries" in the International Folktale Classification System.

**Tellers and their tales in the Gaelic tradition**[42]

"Seán Ó Conaill (1854-1931) lived in County Kerry and was a well-known *sgéalaidhthe*–traditional Gaelic storyteller. When Sean was in his seventies, Séamus Ó Duilearga collected his repertoire, consisting of over 150 folktales and legends, as well as songs, poems, prayers, and other traditional items. Ó Conaill described the 19th and early 20th century storytelling environment:

"When the long nights would come long ago, the people of this and another village would gather together every night sitting beside the fire or wherever they could find room in the house. Many a device they would resort to shorten the night. The man who had a long tale, or the man who had the shorter tales (*eachtraithe*), used to be telling them. At that time, people used to go earning their pay working in County Limerick, County Tipperary and County Cork, and many a tale they had when they would return, everyone with his own story, so that you would not notice the night passing. Often the cock would crow before you would think of going home.

"I used to watch out for anyone with a story, and when the travelers (beggars) would come and one of them would stop in the village, we used to go to the house they stayed listening to them telling stories and trying to pick them up from them. I had only to hear a story once to have it. These 'Finn tales'—nobody knows who made them. We never got any account from anyone when they were made or who composed them. They are very fine things to shorten the night in company especially those which have plenty of action in them, for example, a hero's feats of valour…

"In the beginning of my life when I was growing up I was very interested in the Finn tales (*scéalta fiannaíochta*) if I heard of anyone who could tell them. There was no one very near who could tell them but there was a man in the village called Micheál Ó Conaill, and he used to spend his time after Michaelmas going around the countryside making baskets (*cléibheanna*)—there were few people at that time able to make them—and he used to be away until Christmas. When he came home after his rounds, he had a collection of tales to tell, and I would be well to the fore in the crowd listening to him, and whatever he said I took it from him.

"So as I was growing up and taking things in, if I went out at night with anyone and heard a story, I would want to return again and again if someone would come with me, but those of my own age were not interested in stories; they preferred other kinds of amusement…If I had known thirty years ago [that people would be looking for stories] I would have more of them certainly, but nobody bothered about them, and the pastime then and what has become commonplace for many years past—music, dancing and drinking—makes poor company. Nobody came my way but an occasional withered old man to spend a while [of a night] talking to me."

---

[42] This text is quoted from www.askaboutireland.ie/reading-room/ where it appears under the title above.

# A Great StoryTeller is Dead

By S. Mac G. (Sean Mac Giollarnath)

Sean O'Briain's obituary, published in *The Irish Press*, January 8, 1934

"SEAN O'BRIAIN, storyteller of Loghconeera, Cill Ciarain, Connemara, has died at the age of 82. He was held to have been the greatest of contemporary *sgéalaidhthe*. At three o'clock on the afternoon of New Year's Day he left this life in great peace. He had been ill only a fortnight, he knew that his life was over, and at first was very downcast about parting. He was conscious to the end, and after he had received the Last Sacrament, he became resigned. *Ar dheis Dé go raibh se.*

"To the many who regarded him as the greatest living *sgéalaidhthe*, his death marks the passing of a generation. Irish was his only language. He was in unbroken continuity with the Gaelic past, and his keen brain and richly stored memory made him a man of culture and intelligence who appeared under no handicap for want of English.

"He had never been a man very secure in the wealth of this world, but he was rich in contentment and in the possession of a stock of wonderful tales and of great artistic skill in telling them. One who has seen and heard most of our living storytellers has declared him to have been king of them all. A man of great size and strength in his time he could be as gentle with little children as a mother. His small house was full of grandchildren, all Irish speakers, and lovers of *sgéalaidhtheacht*. It was the old man's chief delight in his very last months to charm these children with his tales of magic and adventure. Like the grandchildren in the Blaskets, their endearing name for grandfather is *daideo*.

"There are still in Connemara large districts where little English is spoken, and there are homes where no English is used. In many homes, storytelling has survived, but it is a rare art and it is only when we hear an accomplished *sgéalidhthe*, such as Sean O Briain, that it comes home to us that this now fugitive art was a highly refined one when Irish culture was a common possession.

"In the telling of his stories, Sean O'Briain became possessed by the spirit and power of their genius. The very flow of the language served him and his delivery in the heroic tales was like that of an actor; he could not pause or suffer interruption to the end of the passage. He recited with great clarity and always as if before a large audience.

"He was entirely free of the pedantry which characterizes some storytellers, and which used to envelop some of the old pipers, but while seemingly unconscious of his art, he displayed it as one who had learned in a school of great traditions. He spoke with great fluency and his tales when written down verbatim had most of the folklore graces, and good literary form. His asides, spoken in undertones, emphasized ironical and humorous situations. The roll of descriptive periods telling of combats of high seas and ships in peril, was given the full note.

**Sean O'Briain, his son Peader (Peter) and family, about 1930**

Source: http://www.oidhreachtlca.ie, "galleries" for photos of O'Briain on this page and on page 55. Peader O'Briain and Annie (Nan) Sullivan were the maternal grandparents of John Mulcahy (a distant cousin) through his mother Bridget, who was one of their eight daughters. John told me that two of his aunts became teachers and four became nurses, defying their poor, rural background.

"His memory was unfailing up to the last month of his life. The recital of a tale of ten thousand words was done without interval or effort, and the words in their sequence were part of the very text of his memory, as were the incidents. It was a great pleasure to hear his humorous tales. In them the storyteller found an unfailing delight which he was able to communicate even to those who had repeatedly heard them. His heroic tales are unexcelled in folklore.

"The way in which he learned the tales illustrates the fugitive life of our language and literature in recent generations. In his youth he used to hear the recitals of his uncle Anthony Conneely, a fisherman (*note from Joyce: and likely brother of Sean's mother, Barbara Conneely*). There was no formal teaching, but the nephew must have had an aptness for memorizing and a keen desire to possess a repertoire that made the older man the admired *racontéur* of fireside gatherings, and in the fishing boat during nights at sea. Anthony Conneely found the traditional grave of many fishermen over thirty years ago, but thanks to Sean O'Briain, his stories have survived. Curtin, the American folklorist, discovered O'Briain over forty years ago and recorded in translation several of his tales, which may be read in English in Curtin's volumes of Irish folklore. Practically all his stories were recorded in Irish by two members of *Institute Béaloideasa*.

"Figures like Sean O'Briain were common to our Irish culture, which is still rapidly perishing. It is in the grand old men of the Gaeltacht that we may see (the old) Gaelic culture. Unfortunately, the importance of *sean-sgéalaidheacht* in the survival of the language has never been fully recognized. The storyteller gave to his hearers a great body of literary language in artistic form, and for them no other form of literature was available, if we accept the songs and *dånta*. The storytellers are going and the recording of their wealth of folklore is urgent. If the revival had, in its early years, seized the colleges and universities, preachers, orators and teachers would have found the best of models in men of the type of this Sean O'Briain.

"It is remarkable that the sections of our race most affected by the economic effects of plantations, clearances, and penal laws are the very people most faithful to our own language and culture. One cannot avoid remembering that the barren rocks of Lochconeera, between the hills and the sea, are not a fitting heritage for people who so nobly cling, in the face of all examples, to the tongue and the culture of their fathers. This notice of the departure of our *sgéalaidhthe* may fittingly close with a note on his way of ending a story. Often, he gave the usual humorous ending, associating himself with the characters of the tale, but frequently he ended with an impressive prayer. It was: *Sin é mo sgéal-sa, Dia le mo bhéal-sa. Tioc-faidh an t-éag, 'S ba mhör an sgéal; Beannacht Dé le hanam na marbh, Amén.* (That's my story, God be with my mouth. Death will come, and that would be a great story. The blessing of God with the souls of the dead." (end of Sean's obituary)

## One of Sean O'Briain's Stories

Sean O'Briain told this story to Jeremiah Curtin, an American folklorist, in 1893 when Sean was 42 years old. This occurred during Curtin's second folklore collecting trip to western Ireland, where he stayed for several months. A year later, Curtin published *Hero Tales of Ireland*, Macmillan and Company, London, 1894, which includes four of O'Briain's stories, including this one on pp. 119-135.

## "The King's Son and the White-Bearded Scolog"
### Transcript of a story told by Sean O'Briain in 1893 and published by Jeremiah Curtin

Not in our time, nor the time of our fathers, but long ago, there lived an old king in Erin. This king had but the one son, and the son had risen up to be a fine strong hero; no man in the kingdom could stand before him in combat. The queen was dead, and the king was gloomy and bitter in himself because old age was on him. The strength had gone from his limbs, and gladness from his heart. No matter what people said, they could not drive sorrow from him.

One day the king called up his son, and this is what he said to him, "You are of age to marry. We cannot tell how long I'll be here, and it would cheer and delight me to see your wife; she might be a daughter to me in my last days."

"I am willing to obey you," said the son; "but I know no woman that I care for. I have never seen anyone that I would marry."

With that, the old king sent for a druid, and said, "You must tell where my son can find the right bride for himself. You must tell us what woman he should marry."

"There is but one woman," said the druid, "who can be the right wife for your son, and she is the youngest daughter of the white-bearded scolog; she is the wisest young woman in the world and has the most power."

"Where does her father live, and how are we to settle it?" asked the king of the druid.

"I have no knowledge of the place where that scolog lives," said the druid, "and there is no one here who knows. Your son must go himself and walk the world till he finds the young woman. If he finds her and gets her, he'll have the best bride that ever came to a king's son."

"I am willing to go in search of the scolog's daughter," said the young man, "and I'll never stop till I find her."

With that, he left his father and the druid, and never stopped till he went to his foster-mother and told her the whole story, told her the wish of his father, and the advice the old druid had given him.

"My three brothers live on the road you must travel," said the foster-mother; "and the eldest one knows how to find that scolog, but without the friendship of all of them, you'll not be able to make the journey. I'll give you something that will gain their good-will for you." With that, she went to an inner room, and made three cakes of flour and baked them. When the three were ready, she brought them out, and gave them to the young man. "When you come to my youngest brother's castle," said she, "he will rush at you to kill you, but strike him on the breast with one of the cakes; that minute he'll be friendly and give you good entertainment. The second brother and the eldest will meet you like the youngest."

On the following morning, the king's son left a blessing with his foster-mother, took one for the road from her, and went away carrying the three cakes with him. He travelled that day with great swiftness over hills and through valleys, past great towns, and small villages, and never stopped nor stayed till he came in the evening to a very large castle. In he went, and inside was a woman before him.

"God save you!" said he to the woman.

"God save yourself!" said she; "and will you tell me what brought you this way, and where are you going?"

"I came here," said the king's son, "to see the giant of this castle, and to speak with him."

"Be said by me," replied the woman, "and go away out of this without waiting for the giant."

"I will not go without seeing him," said the king's son. "I have never set eyes on a giant, and I'll see this one."

"I pity you," said the woman; "your time is short in this life. You'll not be long without seeing the giant, and it's not much you'll see in this world after setting eyes on him; and it would be better for you to take a drink of wine to give you strength before he comes."

The king's son had barely swallowed the wine when he heard a great noise beyond the castle.

"Fee, faw, foh!" roared someone, in a thundering voice.

The king's son looked out; and what should he see but the giant with a shaggy goat going out in front of him and another coming on behind, a dead hag on his shoulder, a great hog of a wild boar under his left arm, and a yellow flea on the club which he held in his right hand before him.

60

"I don't know will I blow you into the air or put my foot on you," said the giant, when he set eyes on the king's son. With that, he threw his load to the ground, and was making at his visitor to kill him when the young man struck the giant on the breast with one of the three cakes which he had from the foster-mother.

That minute the giant knew who was before him, and called out, "Isn't it the fine welcome I was giving my sister's son from Erin?"

With that, he changed entirely, and was so glad to see the king's son that he didn't know what to do for him or where to put him. He made a great feast that evening; the two ate and drank with contentment and delight. The giant was so pleased with the king's son that he took him to his own bed. He wasn't three minutes in the bed when he was sound asleep and snoring. With every breath that the giant took in, he drew the king's son into his mouth and as far as the butt of his tongue; with every breath that he sent out, he drove him to the rafters of the castle, and the king's son was that way going up and down between the bed and the roof until daybreak, when the giant let a breath out of him, and closed his mouth; next moment the king's son was down on his lips.

"What are you doing to me?" cried the giant.

"Nothing," said the king's son; "but you didn't let me close an eye all the night. With every breath you let out of you, you drove me up to the rafters; and with every breath you took in, you drew me into your mouth and as far as the butt of your tongue."

"Why didn't you wake me?"

"How could I wake you when time failed me to do it?"

"Oh, then, sister's son from Erin," said the giant, "it's the poor night's rest I gave you; but if you had a bad bed, you must have a good breakfast." With that, the giant rose, and the two ate the best breakfast that could be had out of Erin.

After breakfast, the king's son took the giant's blessing with him, and left his own behind. He travelled all that day with great speed and without halt or rest, till he came in the evening to the castle of the second giant. In front of the door was a pavement of sharp razors, edges upward, a pavement which no man could walk on. Long, poisonous needles, set as thickly as bristles in a brush, were fixed, points downward, under the lintel of the door, and the door was low. The king's son went in with one start over the razors and under the needles, without grazing his head or cutting his feet. When inside, he saw a woman before him.

"God save you!" said the king's son.

"God save yourself!" said the woman.

The same conversation passed between them then as passed between himself and the woman in the first castle.

"God help you!" said the woman when she heard his story. "'Tis not long you'll be alive after the giant comes. Here's a drink of wine to strengthen you."

Barely had he the wine swallowed when there was a great noise behind the castle, and the next moment the giant came in with a thundering and rattling.

"Who is this that I see?" asked he, and with that, he sprang at the stranger to put the life out of him; but the king's son struck him on the breast with the second cake which he got from his foster-mother.

That moment the giant knew him, and called out, "A strange welcome I had for you, sister's son from Erin, but you'll get good treatment from me now." The giant and the king's son made three parts of that night. One part they spent in telling tales, the second in eating and drinking, and the third in sound, sweet slumber.

Next morning the young man went away after breakfast, and never stopped until he came to the castle of the third giant; and a beautiful castle it was, thatched with the down of cotton grass, the roof was as white as milk, beautiful to look at from afar or nearby. The third giant was as angry at meeting him as the other two; but when he was struck in the breast with the third cake, he was as kind as the best man could be. When they had taken supper together, the giant said to his sister's son, "Will you tell me what journey you are on?"

"1 will, indeed," said the king's son; and he told his whole story from beginning to end.

"It is well that you told me," said the giant, "for I can help you; and if you do what I tell, you'll finish your journey in safety. At midday to-morrow you will come to a lake; hide in the rushes that are growing at one side of the water. You will not be long there when twelve swans will alight near the rushes and take the crests from their heads; with that, the swan skins will fall from them, and they will rise up the most beautiful women that you have ever set eyes on. When they go into bathe, take the crest of the youngest, put it in your bosom next the skin, take the eleven others and hold them in your hand. When the young women come out, give the eleven crests to their owners; but when the twelfth comes, you'll not give her the crest unless she carries you to her father's castle in Ardilawn Dreeachta (High Island of Enchantment). She will refuse, and say that strength fails her to carry you, and she will beg for the crest. Be firm and keep it in your bosom; never give it up till she promises to take you. She will do that when she sees there is no help for it."

Next morning the king's son set out after breakfast, and at midday he was hidden in the rushes. He was barely there when the swans came. Everything happened as the giant had said, and the king's son followed his counsels.

When the twelve swans came out of the lake, he gave the eleven crests to the older ones, but kept the twelfth, the crest of the youngest, and gave it only when she promised to carry him to her father's. The moment she put the crest on her head, she was in love with the king's son. When she came in sight of the island, however much she loved him when they started from the lakeside, she loved him twice as much now. She came to the ground at some distance from the castle, and said to the young man at parting,

"Thousands of king's sons and champions have come to give greeting to my father at the door of his castle, but every man of them perished. You will be saved if you obey me. Stand with your right foot inside the threshold and your left foot outside; put your head under the lintel. If your head is inside, my father will cut it from your shoulders; if it is outside, he will cut it off also. If it is under the lintel when you cry 'God save you!' he'll let you go in safety."

They parted there; she went to her own place, and he went to the scolog's castle, put his right foot inside the threshold, his left foot outside, and his head under the lintel. "God save you!" called he to the scolog.

"A blessing on you!" cried the scolog, "but my curse on your teacher. I'll give you lodgings tonight, and I'll come to you myself in the morning;" and with that he sent a servant with the king's son to a building outside. The servant took a bundle of straw with some turf and potatoes, and, putting these down inside the door, said, "Here are bed, supper, and fire for you."

The king's son made no use of food or bed, and he had no need of them, for the scolog's daughter came soon after, spread a cloth, took a small bundle from her pocket, and opened it. That moment the finest food and drink were there before them. The king's son ate and drank with relish, and good reason he had after the long journey. When supper was over, the young woman whittled a small shaving from a staff which she brought with her; and that moment the finest bed that any man could have was there in the room.

"I will leave you now," said she; "my father will come early in the morning to give you a task. Before he comes, turn the bed over; 'twill be a shaving again, and then you can throw it into the fire. I will make you a new bed to-morrow." With that, she went away, and the young man slept till daybreak. Up he sprang, then turned the bed over, made a shaving of it, and burned it.

It was not long till the scolog came, and this is what he said to the king's son, "I have a task for you today, and I hope you will be able to do it. There is a lake on my land not far from this, and a swamp at one side of it. You are to drain that lake and dry the swamp for me, and have the work finished this evening; if not, I will take the head from you at sunset. To drain the lake, you are to dig through a neck of land two miles in width; here is a good spade, and I'll show you the place where you're to use it."

The king's son went with the scolog, who showed the ground, and then left him. "What am I to do?" said the king's son. "Sure, a thousand men couldn't dig that land out in ten years, working night and day; how am I to do it between this and sunset?" However it was, he began to dig; but if he did, for every sod he threw out, seven sods came in, and soon he saw that, in place of mending his trouble, 'twas making it worse he was. He cast aside the spade then, sat down on the sod heap, and began to lament. He wasn't long there when the scolog's daughter came with a cloth in her hand and the small bundle in her pocket.

"Why are you lamenting there like a child?" asked she of the king's son.

"Why shouldn't I lament when the head will be taken from me at sunset?"

"'Tis a longtime from this to sunset. Eat your breakfast first of all; see what will happen then," said she. Taking out the little bundle, she put down before him the best breakfast a man could have. While he was eating, she took the spade, cut out one sod, and threw it away. When she did that, every spadeful of earth in the neck of land followed the first spadeful; the whole neck of land was gone, and before midday there wasn't a spoonful of water in the lake or the swamp, the whole place was dry.

"You have your head saved to-day, whatever you'll do tomorrow," said she, and she left him.

Toward evening the scolog came, and, meeting the king's son, cried out, "You are the best man that ever came the way, or that ever I expected to look at." The king's son went to his lodging. In the evening, the scolog's daughter came with supper and made a bed for him as good as the first one. Next morning the king's son rose at daybreak, destroyed his bed, and waited to see what would happen.

The scolog came early, and said, "1 have a field outside, a mile long and a mile wide, with a very tall tree in the middle of it. Here are two wedges, a sharp axe, and a fine new drawing knife. You are to cut down the tree and make from it barrels to cover the whole field. You are to make the barrels and fill them with water before sunset, or the head will be taken from you."

The king's son went to the field, faced the tree, and gave it a blow with his axe; but if he did, the axe bounded back from the trunk, struck him on the forehead, stretched him on the flat of his back, and raised a lump on the place where it hit him. He gave three blows, was served each time in the same way, and had three lumps on his forehead. He was rising from the third blow, the life almost gone from him, and he crying bitterly, when the scolog's daughter came with his breakfast. While he was eating the breakfast, she struck one little chip from the tree; that chip became a barrel, and then the whole tree turned into barrels, which took their places in rows, and covered the field. Between the rows there was just room for a man to walk. Not a barrel but was filled with water.

From a chip she had in her hand, the young woman made a wooden dipper, from another chip she made a pail, and said to the king's son, "You'll have these in your two hands, and be walking up and down between the rows of barrels, putting a little water into this and a little into that barrel. When my father comes, he will see you at the work and invite you to the castle to-night, but you are not to go with him. You will say that you are content to lodge tonight where you lodged the other nights."

With that, she went away, and the king's son was going around among the barrels pouring a little water into one and another of them, when the scolog came. "You have the work done," said he, "and you must come to the castle for the night."

"1 am well satisfied to lodge where I am, and to sleep as I slept since I came here," said the young man, and the scolog left him.

The young woman brought the supper and gave a fresh bed. Next morning the scolog came the third time, and said, "Come with me now; I have a third task for you." With that, the two went to a quarry. "Here are tools," said the scolog, pointing to a crowbar, a pickaxe, a trowel, and every implement used in quarrying and building. "You are to quarry stones today and build between this and sunset the finest and largest castle in the world, with outhouses and stables, with cellars and kitchens. There must be cooks, with men and women to serve; there must be dishes and utensils of every kind and furniture of every description; not a thing is to be lacking, or the head will go from you this evening at sunset."

The scolog went home; and the king's son began to quarry with crowbar and pickaxe, and though he worked hard, the morning was far gone when he had three small pieces of stone quarried. He sat down to lament.

"Why are you lamenting this morning?" asked the scolog's daughter, who came now with his breakfast.

"Why shouldn't I lament when the head will be gone from me this evening? I am to quarry stones and build the finest castle in the world before sunset. Ten thousand men couldn't do the work in ten years."

"Take your breakfast," said the young woman; "you'll see what to do after that."

64

While he was eating, she quarried one stone; and the next moment every stone in the quarry that was needed took its place in the finest and largest castle ever built, with outhouses and cellars and kitchens. A moment later, all the people were there, men and women, with utensils of all kinds. Everything was finished but a small spot at the principal fireplace.

"The castle is ready," said the scolog's daughter; "your head will stay with you today, and there are no more tasks before you at present. Here is a trowel and mortar; you will be finishing this small spot at the fire when my father comes. He will invite you to his castle tonight, and you are to go with him this time. After dinner, he will seat you at a table, and throw red wheat on it from his pocket. I have two sisters older than I am; they and I will fly in and alight on the table in the form of three pigeons, and we'll be eating the wheat; my father will tell you to choose one of his three daughters to marry. You'll know me by this: there will be a black quill in one of my wings. I'll show it; choose me."

All happened as the scolog's daughter said; and when the king's son was told to make his choice in the evening, he chose the pigeon that he wanted. The three sprang from the table, and when they touched the floor, they were three beautiful women. A priest and a clerk were brought to the castle, and the two were married that evening.

A month passed in peace and enjoyment; but the king's son wished to go back now to Erin to his father. He told the wife what he wanted; and this is what she said to him, "My father will refuse you nothing. He will tell you to go, though he doesn't wish to part with you. He will give you his blessing; but this is all pretense, for he will follow us to kill us. You must have a horse for the journey, and the right horse. He will send a man with you to three fields. In the first field are the finest horses that you have ever laid eyes on; take none of them. In the second field are splendid horses, but not so fine as in the first field; take none of these either. In the third field, in the farthest corner, near the river, is a long-haired, shaggy, poor little old mare; take that one. The old mare is my mother. She has great power, but not so much as my father, who made her what she is, because she opposed him. I will meet you beyond the hill and we shall not be seen from the castle."

The king's son brought the mare; and when they mounted her, wings came from her sides, and she was the grandest steed ever seen. Away she flew over mountains, hills, and valleys, till they came to the seashore, and then they flew over the sea.

When the servant man went home, and the scolog knew what horse they had chosen, he turned himself and his two daughters into red fire and shot after the couple. No matter how swiftly the mare moved, the scolog travelled faster, and was coming up. When the three reached the opposite shore of the sea, the daughter saw her father coming, and turned the mare into a small boat, the king's son into a fisherman, and made a fishing-rod of herself. Soon the scolog came, and his two daughters with him.

"Have you seen a man and a woman passing the way riding on a mare?" asked he of the fisherman.

"I have," said the fisherman. "You'll soon overtake them."

On went the scolog; and he never stopped till he raced around the whole world and came back to his own castle. "Oh, then, we were the fools," said the scolog to his daughters. "Sure, they were the fisherman, the boat, and the rod."

Off they went a second time in three balls of red fire; and they were coming near again when the scolog's youngest daughter made a spinning-wheel of her mother, a bundle of flax of herself, and an old woman of her husband. Up rushed the scolog, and spoke to the spinner, "Have you seen a mare pass the way and two on her back?" asked he.

"I have, indeed," said the old woman; "and she is not far ahead of you."

Away rushed the scolog; and he never stopped till he raced around the whole world and came back to his own castle a second time. "Oh, but we were the fools!" said the scolog. "Sure, they were the old woman with the spinning-wheel and the flax, and they are gone from us now; for they are in Erin, and we cannot take our power over the border, nor work against them unless they are outside of Erin. There is no use in our following them; we might as well stay where we are."

The scolog and his daughters remained in the castle at Ardilawn of Enchantment; but the king's son rode home on the winged mare, with his wife on a pillion behind him. When near the castle of the old king in Erin, the couple dismounted, and the mare took her own form of a woman. She could do that in Erin. The three never stopped till they went to the old king. Great was the welcome before them; and if ever there was joy in a castle, there was joy then."

## The Magic Cup

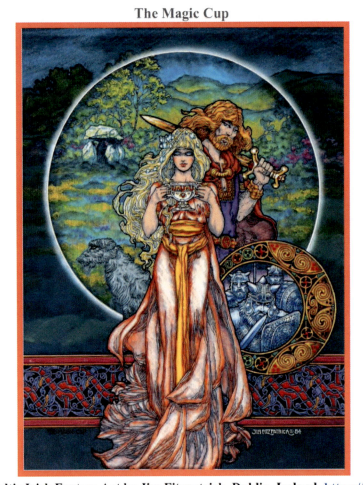

**Contemporary Celtic Irish Fantasy Art by Jim Fitzpatrick, Dublin, Ireland, https://jimfitzpatrick.com**

# Appendix Six

## Loughaconeera School Children's Story Collection, 1937-1938

The Irish National Folklore Collection of 1937 and 1938 provides valuable information about 19th century life through its Schools Collection.[44] Throughout Ireland, teachers asked students to collect stories and folklore from family and neighbors about earlier times. Students at the National School at Loughaconeera[45] collected 46 stories, written in Irish. I hired an Irish translator, Bridget Anne Hughes of Translations.ie, to select and translate several stories to include in this essay.

Bridget Anne emailed the following to me on 30 June 2021: "Four of the stories have been received from Seán O'Brien (storyteller) and collected by Mary O'Brien. The stories I have read so far are fables that would have been passed down through the generations in the folklore tradition. They don't refer to local people or places but are a Connemara version of Aesop's Fables. The Irish language in the stories is older and more obscure than modern-day Irish because it comes from the oral storytelling tradition of that time. They are not all complete, and a few words are missing, but the stories can be understood.

"I read all 46 stories from the Loughaconeera School Collection. I had hoped that some would mention the local area or the names of your ancestors (on the Joyce/O'Brien family tree), but they all appear to be 'hero tales' and mention neither the local area nor any specific person. They are beautiful stories in the Irish folklore tradition and well put together but may not be exactly what you need for your family history." (End of 30 June 2021 email from Bridget Anne Hughes).

**I asked Bridget Anne to select and translate from Irish to English two of the four tales collected from Sean O'Briain by Mary O'Briain, a student at the School and likely one of Sean's many granddaughters.**

### Sean O'Briain's first School Collection story, transcribed by Mary O'Briain: Scéal Sheáinín

Bhí fear ann fadó is sé an t-ainm bhí air Seáinín. Lá amháin bhí Seáinín ag dul ag pósadh, is fuair a mháthair go leor rudaí deasa dhó. Fuair sí cearc is bhruith sí í. Ansin dubhairt sí le Seáinín "rachaidh mise ag iarraidh na mná agus an tsagairt dhuit". "Tá go maith" adeir Seáinín. "Anois cuirfidh mé an chearc síos ag rósta is ná leig di dóghadh". D'imthigh an mháthair ag iarraidh an tsagairt agus na mná. Thug Seáinín aire don chearc ar feadh tamaill. Ansin tháinic dúil aige sa gcearc agus adeir sé "tá ceathramha den chearc soe dul domsa agus íosfaidh mé é. Tá ceathramha eile ag dul don tsagart agus is fearr an aghaidh orm féin é ná air"

---

[43] Derryrush Townland shares a border with the northeastern border of Loughaconeera.

[44] The Folklore Collection is housed at the University College Dublin. Only the Schools Collection is digitized.

[45] The first National School in Loughaconeera was built in the late 19th century. The school participated in the National Folklore Collection program. Stories collected from Loughaconeera are at http://www.duchas.ie/ga/cbes/46026a96. Before National Schools opened, Catholic students attended small, informal, illegal "hedge" schools (in private homes and barns) because Penal Laws only allowed schools of the Anglican faith (Church of England/Ireland). Penal Laws deprived Irish Catholics of many rights, including education for their children, unless they converted.

agus d'ith sé an piosa bhí dul don tsagart. "Tá ceathramha eile ag dul go mo mhnaoi is, is fearr léithe mise dhá ithe ná í féin" agus d'ith sé an ceathramha bhí dhul dá mhnaoi. "Anois" adeir sé "níl fágthaagam ach an ceathrú tá dul go mo mháthair agus ó tharla go bhfuil an aois uirthi agus na fiacla go dona aici níl sí indon é congailt agus mar sin íosfaidh mé féin é." Nuair a bhí sí ite aige tháinic aithmhéala air is dubhairt sé cá bhfuighe mé cearc le haghaidh an dream tá amuigh.

Annsin chuimhnigh sé air féin go raibh cearc ag gor ag a mháthair. Rug sé uirthi agus thug sé anuas í is chaith sé síos sa bpota í. Thosuigh sé ag ól an barraille leana agus is gearr go raibh sé tuirseach. Ansin bhreathnuigh sé amach go bhfeicfeadh a raibh a mháthair ag tigheacht ach ní raibh. Nuair a bhreathnuigh sé isteach chonnaic sé an barraille leanna doirte ag an ngadhar. "Anois" adeir sé "níl blas fágtha sa teach agam, agus tá an t-urlár fliuch agam. Ach má tá féin ní i bhfad bheidh sé mar sin mar tá mala plúir ansin agus craitheadh mé air é. Tá an cearc crochta áll agam is caillfear na héanacha ach gabhfadh mé féin ar gor orthu is déarfadh mé le mo mháthair nuair thiocfas sí ag an doras, glug, glug a mháithrín tá Seainín ar na huibheacha". Nuair a tháinic an mháthair is an criú bhí i n-éineacht léithe "hóra a Sheáinín" adeir sí . "Glug glug a mháithrín tá Seáinín ar na huibheacha." Nuair a chonaic a mháthair is an bhean an chaoi bhí ar an teach bhí siad as a gcéill is chuaidh bean Sheáinín abhaile arís.

### Sean O'Briain's first School Collection story, translated by Bridget Anne Hughes: Seáinín's Story

There was a man long ago and his name was Seáinín. One day Seáinín was going to get married, and his mother found him many nice things. She found a chicken and boiled it. Then she told Seáinín "I'll go and get the bride and the priest for you". "All right," said Seáinín. "Now I'll put the chicken down to roast and don't let it burn." The mother went looking for the priest and the bride. Seáinín took care of the hen for a while. Then he had a craving for the hen and said "a quarter of this chicken is for me, and I will eat it. There is another quarter for the priest, and I have a better face myself than him" and he ate the piece that was for the priest. "Another quarter is for my bride and she'd rather I eat two than have one for herself," and he ate the quarter that was for his bride. "Now," he said, "I have only the quarter left for my mother and since she is old and has bad teeth she is not able to chew so I will eat it myself." When he had eaten it, he regretted it and wondered where he would find a chicken for his mother and bride.

Then he remembered that his mother had a hatching hen. He grabbed it, killed it, and threw it into the pot. He started drinking the barrel of ale and it wasn't long until he was tired. Then he looked out to see if his mother was coming but she was not. When he looked inside, he saw that the dog had spilled the barrel of beer. "Now." he said, "I have nothing left in the house, and I have a wet floor. But even if it is, it won't be long like that because there's a bag of flour to shake on it. I have killed the hatching hen and the chicks will die but I will hatch them myself and I'll tell my mother when she comes to the door. Glug, glug, mother, Seáinín is on the eggs." When the mother arrived, "Hello Seáinín," she said. "Glug glug, mother, Seáinín is on the eggs." When his mother and his bride saw the state of the house, they were alarmed and angry and Seáinín's bride went back home.

### Sean O'Briain's second School Collection story, transcribed by Mary O'Briain: Seán an tSléibhe

Bhí dhá cheannuighe ann fadó agus sé an t-ainm a bhí ortha an Ceannuighe beag ruadh agus an Ceannuigh mór ruadh. Bhí fear eile ann agus sé an t-ainm a bhí air Seán an t-Sléibhe agus bhíodh an da cheannuighe ag dealál leis go minic. Bhí giorrán ag Seán agus ba mhaith leis é a dhíol. Lá amháin tháinich na ceannuighe cuige agus d'fhiafhruigh siad de a ndíolfeadh sé an giorrán dubhairt sé go ndiolfeadh. D'fhiafhruigh siad de cé méad a bheadh sé ag iarraidh ar an ngiorrán.

"O! ní dhíolfann mó ghiorrán ar dhá chéad phunt," adéir Seán, "mar cuile uair a bhuailfeas tú buille de mhaide air tiubhraidh sé lth. chr. duit." D'imthigh na ceannuigthe annsan agus dubhairt siad go dtiocfadh siad arís agus go dtiubhraidh an t-airgead leó. Nuair a fuair Seán imthighthe iad thug sé ceiléar bran do'n chapall agus chuir sé trí phíosa lth. chr. tríd dó agus sluig sé iad leis an mbran.

Is gearr in dhiadh sin go dtáinich na ceannuighthe agus an t-airgead aca le haghaidh an giorrán a cheannacht. "Tiubhraidh muid céad punt ar an ngiorrán," adeir na ceannuigthe. Thugadar an céad punt do Sheán agus thugadar an giorrán leó. "Coinneóchaidh mise an giorrán anocht agus béidh mé saidhbhir ar maidin," dubhairt duine aca. Nuair a tháinich an oidhche chuir an an ceannuighe isteach an giorrán i sgioból agus thosuigh sé ag bualadh an ghiorráin. Chaith sé dá lth. chr cuige ach sin é an méid dá marbhochthaí é.

Chuaidh na ceannuighthe go dtí Seán an céad lá eile le haghaidh é a marbhugad. Nuair a tháinigh na ceannuigthe isteach - tosuig Seán agus a bhean ag troid, mar budh eadh. Dheamhan blás a rinne Seán, ach rasúr a fhághail agus í a thairringt ar mhuinéal a mná agus tháinich go leor fuil amach. "A Diabhail", adéir an ceannuigh "tá do bhean marbh agat." Ní túisge liomsa mó bhean a mharbhadh ná í a dhéanamh beó. Fuair sé adharch ón ráta agus chuir i mbéal a mná í, agus dubhairt sé leithí "Éirig go beó." Déirigh an bhean. "Ó," adeir an ceannuigh, "an dtiubharfá an adharc sin dhomsa agus maithfidh mé do chionnta dhuit." "Tiubhrad," adéir Seán. Nuair a tháinich an ceannuigh abhaile mharbh sé a bhean agus chuir sé an adharc ina béal agus dubhairt sé leithí, "Éirigh go beó" (a dubhairt an ceannuig). Ach níor éirigh mar bhí si marbh in dá ríríbh.

Chuaidh an ceannuighe go dtí Seán agus fearg air. An tam a dtáinic sé bhí Seán ag obair inaice locha agus ba lá ann bhréagh a bhí ann. Bhí beithidhigh Sheáin go léir cruinnigthe ar bhruach na locha agus bhí a sgáile san uisge. Sé an chéad rud a d'fhiafhruigh an ceannuighe de Sheán cé fhuair sé an méid sin beithidheach. Dubhairt sé gur sa loch a fuair sé iad, agus geobhfadh tusa thú fhéin beithidhigh mar iad má theigheann tú síos san loch. "Gabhaidh" adéir an ceannuighe. Thug sé léim agus chuaidh sé amach i lár na locha. Nuair a bhí an ceannuighe ag dul síos déirigh súilíní agus torann ar an uisge. D'fhiafhruigh an ceannuighe beag ruadh de Sheán céard a bhí an duine eile a rádh. "Deir sé go bhfuil tusa i gcolbha an aonaigh agus é féin i lár an aonaigh agus é a leanamhaint." Chuaidh an ceannuigh eile amach in dhiadh agus báthadh an bheirt aca. Bhí Seán áthasach deire a bheith leis an mbeirt."

## Sean O'Briain's 2<u>nd</u> School Collection story, trans. by Bridget Anne Hughes: Seán of the Mountain

Once upon a time there were two merchants and they were called the little red-haired merchant and the big red-haired merchant. There was another man by the name of Seán of the Mountain and the two merchants often traded with him. Seán had a gelding to sell. One day the merchants asked him if he would sell the gelding and he said that he would. They asked him how much he wanted for the gelding.

"Oh! I wouldn't sell my gelding for two hundred pounds," said Seán, "because every time you hit him with a stick he'll give you half a crown." The merchants left then and said that they would come back and bring the money with them. When Seán got them gone he gave the horse a basin of bran and mixed three half-crown coins through it and the horse swallowed them along with the bran.

Shortly afterwards the merchants arrived with the money to buy the gelding. "We'll give you a hundred pounds for the gelding." said the merchants. They gave John the hundred pounds and took the gelding with them. "I'll keep the gelding tonight and I'll be rich in the morning," one of them said. When night came, the merchant put the gelding in a barn and began to beat it. The gelding produced two half-crown coins but that was all the money he gave even if the merchant was to kill him.

The merchants went to Seán the next day to kill him. When the merchants came in, Seán and his wife pretended to start fighting. Seán got a razor and put it against his wife's neck and a lot of blood came out. "You devil," said the merchant, "you've killed your wife." "I'd no sooner kill my wife than bring her back to life." He got a horn from the ram and put it in his wife's mouth and said to her, "Get up fast." The woman got up. "Oh," said the merchant, "would you give me that horn and I will forgive you for your offences." "I'll give it to you," said Seán. When the merchant went home, he killed his wife and put the horn in her mouth and told her, "Get up fast." But she didn't get up because she was dead.

The merchant went to Seán, and he was furious. When he arrived, Seán was working by a lake, and it was a beautiful fine day. All of Seán's cattle were gathered on the shore of the lake and their shadows could be seen in the water. The first thing the merchant asked Seán was how did he get so many cattle. Seán said that he found them in the lake, and the merchant would find cattle like them if he went down into the lake. "I will," said the merchant. He took a leap and went out into the middle of the lake. As the merchant went down there were bubbles and noise on the water. The little red-haired merchant asked Seán what the other man was saying. "He says you are in the corner of the fair and he is in the middle of the fair and you should follow him." The other merchant followed him and both of them drowned. Seán was happy to see the end of the two of them.

# Appendix Seven

## 19th century Lives of County Galway Farmer-fishermen Families[46]

**Claddagh fishwife in red petticoat and cape, curraghs, and Claddagh fisherman, about 1870**

In Loughaconeera and Rosmuc, men were farmer-fisherman because they lived near the sea and Connemara soil is rocky and poor. Most families owned a curragh and depended upon coastal fishing for their food and livelihood. The 1836 Irish Fisheries Inquiry Report noted that from Killary to Spiddal in Connemara, there were 1,236 rowing boats, 316 open sail boats (like the Galway hooker), 111 half-decked boats, and one fully decked sailboat. In addition to fishing, most families kept gardens, pigs, chickens, a donkey or horse, cows, and goats. Until the mid- to late-19th century, farm animals were kept in the house during the winter to help warm the family.

In 1854, the *Ulster Journal of Archelogy* published a study[47] of Claddagh,[48] a traditional Connemara fishing village, describing fishermen's lives on Galway Bay and its many inlets. "There are no braver men at sea (than men from Claddagh) when they go forth with their priestly benediction, and the blessing of salt and ashes. They would not commence the fishing season until a priest blessed the bay. They will not put to sea if a hare appears to them, and the whole fleet has been known to return home, without dropping a line, because a boy called out that he had seen a hare. No boat goes to sea without oat-cake, salt and ashes…. they consider there is a blessing in these things. If a crow flies over the boat, and croaks as he passes, it is a good omen.

---

[46] For "Highlights of Galway City's Early History," see Appendix Nine, page 79.

[47] Retrieved from https://thewildgeese.irish/profiles/blogs/a-19th-century-account-of-the-claddagh.

[48] Claddagh was located just outside the medieval walls of Galway City. Following a 1930 outbreak of tuberculosis in Claddagh, all of the old stone and thatched cottages were destroyed, and the land was absorbed into Galway City.

"When a boat comes in with fish, the boatman gives a fish to every beggar who may be there to ask… it would be most unlucky to refuse charity out of what God sent to the net. This custom has been dying out with the increase of pauperism, the opening of the poor house and railway, and the many mouths that must be filled with fish in Dublin. The custom is, in my mind, proof that in old times, there could not have been anything like the present amount of beggary in the district.

"For generations, the Claddagh was home to an impressive fleet of fishing boats, and an impressive crew of men who manned them. The women would take the day's catch across the river to the open-air fish market where the fish would be laid down on cobblestones for display. You would see only women carrying baskets and bargaining with customers, all in Irish." (End of excerpt.)

Hookers and smaller working boats also transported goods along the west coast. Men transported turf[48] from Connemara, where it was plentiful, to the Aran Islands. They returned with cattle, limestone, and supplies for Connemara merchants. Fishing communities along Galway Bay prospered until the early 1800s, when herring left the area, causing fishing villages to decline.

From the 1880s, west Galway fishermen no longer had exclusive access to local fisheries. In 1905 alone, 440 steam-propelled Scottish boats worked Irish waters with little concern for sustainability. Even after large foreign boats became common, the local west Galway fishing industry did not modernize until well after the 1890s due to poverty and the lack of capital for improvements in ports, vessels, gear, education, and transportation. This caused a rift between local farmer- fishermen and large-scale commercial fishing companies from outside Ireland. At the same time, several British commissions examined the Irish fishing industry and concluded that there was an abundance of fish with no danger of overfishing

Eventually, the west Galway fishing industry declined due to foreign competition; disruption of fish spawning grounds; irregular migration of herring and mackerel; lack of local fish markets; insufficient investment in boats, equipment and harbors; fishermen's loans and subsequent debts; and consistently inadequate government responses to these problems. The mismanagement of commercial fishing in the west of Ireland reflected many factors, including Britain's increased need for protein; technological developments that allowed greater fish catch by fishermen from elsewhere; and the British government's policy of exploiting Ireland to benefit Britain.

Meanwhile, during the 1845-1852 Potato Famine, Anglo and Anglo-Irish landlords evicted Irish tenants throughout Ireland. There is evidence of a single eviction on the Lynch's estate which included Loughaconeera and seven nearby townlands, but there may have been others. Perhaps the Lynch family was more sympathetic to their tenants than other landlords particularly those who never lived in Ireland.[50]

---

[49] "Turf" is the Irish term for "peat," the main fuel across Ireland from pre-historic times until the mid-20th century. Peat forms in bogs from decaying vegetation and is cut into logs for building and burning.

[50] See Appendix Eight, page 74 for a discussion of the Lynches of Barna, County Galway.

The Loughaconeera Heritage Website, at http://www.oidhreachtlca.ie/index.php, reports the following evictions on estates in West County Galway that were nearby but not owned by the Lynches: "On the 17th of September, Mr. John Robertson, agent to the mortgagees of the Martin estates, accompanied by sixty bailiffs, proceeded to the townland of Derryrush[50] [Galway], and evicted seven families comprising forty-two individuals. The houses were levelled on the instant without the slightest opposition being offered by the evicted.

"On Nov. 11th, the same party went upon the islands of Dooletter, and evicted two families consisting of ten persons. Nov. 16th, the same party visited the Townlands of Mace and Dooreher, and evicted seventeen families, comprising one hundred persons, and levelled the houses. Nov. 21 the same party proceeded to the town land of Atry and evicted seventeen families, comprising sixty-five persons, and unroofed the houses. On the 22nd of November, the same party went to the townlands of Cashel, Doonreageran, Rossroe and Glynsk, and evicted sixteen families, comprising eighty-seven human beings, and levelled their houses." *Galway Vindicator*, December 4th, 1851.

# Appendix Eight

## The Lynches of Barna House–History of their County Galway Estate[51]

**Marcus Lynch, 19th c. Loughaconeera landowner    Barna House, home of the Lynches until 1930**
Photos from the National University of Galway, Landed Estates Database

Griffith's Valuation of 1857 identified Nicholas Lynch as the owner of Loughaconeera and adjacent townlands. In 1869, documents identified Marcus Lynch as the owner when he put the estate up for sale (see page 24). When I searched on the Web for the 19th century Lynches of Galway, I located a 19th century family in County Galway with father Nicholas and son Marcus of the right age, time, and place. They resided in Barna, a few miles west of Galway City. Like other landowning gentry, the genealogy of the Lynches is well documented to the 13th century.

There were several dozen Lynch families in Counties Galway, Mayo, Meath, and elsewhere in Ireland in the 19th century who descended from Anglo-Normans and possibly Celts. The Lynches of County Galway descended from Anglo-Normans, mainly from Wales, who conquered the Province of Connacht in 1235. They spoke a Norman dialect of French, which was gradually replaced by Gaelic, then English. Scholars have not identified the earliest ancestors of the Lynches of Galway, but they know that Thomas Lynch, the provost of Galway in 1274, married Bridget, daughter of the Lord Marshall, in 1280. They had two sons, James and William, from whom Galway Lynches are descended. The Lynches held the mayoralty of Galway on more than 80 occasions between 1485 and 1654.

---

[51] The sources for this essay include *Genealogy of the Anglo-Norman Lynches who settled in Galway*, Paul B. McNulty, National University of Ireland Diploma in Genealogy/Family History, 2013; *Burkes' Landed Gentry of Ireland;* and Marcus Lynch of Barna in the *Library of 19th Century Photography*. Normans were Vikings who settled in NW France during the 10th and 11th centuries and later migrated to England and Wales, among other places.

### LYNCH OF BARNA.

MARCUS NICHOLAS LYNCH, of Barna, co. Galway, J.P., D.L., High Sheriff 1869, formerly Lieut. 33rd Regt., *b.* 12 Sept. 1836; *m.* 8 May, 1867, Blanche (*d.* 18 May, 1908), only dau. of Count Juliuz Marylski, of Leuczyca, Duchy of Posen, Poland, and had issue,

1. NICHOLAS MARCUS, *b.* 16 April, 1868, Capt. S. Lanc. Regt., served in W. Africa (medal and clasps), S. Africa (including relief of Ladysmith) (medal and clasps), *d.* on active service 1900, *unm.*
2. John Arthur, *b.* 5 July, 1874; *d. unm.* 25 June, 1892.
1. Ida, a nun.           2. Ethel, a nun.
3. Violet, a nun.

**Lineage.**—The greater portion of the Barna property came into the Lynch family by the marriage of the direct ancestor of the present proprietor with the heir of the O'HALLORANS, the foundations of whose castle are still to be seen.

MARCUS LYNCH, of Barna, descended from the marriage of William Lynch and the heir of O'Halloran, *m.* 1684, Elizabeth, dau. of Oliver Browne, of Coolaron, and was father of

NICHOLAS LYNCH, of Barna, *m.* 1719, Mary, dau. and heir of Neptune Lynch, of Lettermullin, co. Galway. Their only son,

MARCUS LYNCH, of Barna, *m.* 1st, 1742, Anstace (who *d.* March, 1766), dau. of Maurice Blake, of Ballinafad, co. Mayo (*see that family*), and had issue, with three daus. (of whom Julia, *m.* 1784, Hyacinth D'Arcy, of Kiltulla), two sons, the younger of whom, James, *d.* leaving one dau. and heir, who *m.* Maurice Blake, of Ballinafad, co. Mayo. Mr. Lynch *m.* 2ndly, 2 Jan. 1767, Surna, only dau. of Patrick French, of Cloghballymore. His will, dated 28 Nov. 1787, was proved 6 July, 1795. He was *s.* by his elder son,

NICHOLAS LYNCH, of Barna, *m.* 1765, Catherine, only dau. and heir of Henry Blake, of Ballinahill, co. Galway, 2nd son of Blake, of Lehinch, co. Mayo, and by her had one son with five daus., of whom the eldest *m.* 1800, Lawrence Comyn, of Woodstock and Kilcorney (*see that family*).

MARCUS BLAKE LYNCH, of Barna, *m.* 1st, Jan. 1792, Jane Mary, dau. of Mark Byrne, of Mullinahack, Dublin; and 2ndly, 1796, Catherine, 2nd dau. of John Segrave, of Cabra, co. Dublin (*see that family*), by whom at his death, Jan. 1829, he left issue, five daus. (Catherine, Jane, Frances, Clarinda, and Henrietta) and an only son,

NICHOLAS LYNCH, of Barna, D.L., High Sheriff of Galway 1843, *b.* 22 Feb. 1804; *m.* 24 Nov. 1835, Eliza, 2nd dau. of Stephen Grehan, of Rutland Square, Dublin, by Margaret his wife, dau. of George Ryan, of Inch (*see that family*), and by her (who *d.* 10 March, 1857) had issue,

MARCUS NICHOLAS, now of Barna.
Margaret.

Mr. Lynch *d.* 22 Nov. 1862.

**Seat**—Barna, Galway.

According to Burke's *Landed Gentry of Ireland*, reported in the *Landed Estates Database, National University of Ireland, Galway*, "the Lynches acquired the Barna estate through marriage to an O'Halloran heiress in 1684. Further additions were made through marriages and purchases. The Lynches resided at Barna House, described by historian James Hardiman in the 1800s as the 'highly improved and elegant seat of Marcus Blake Lynch which for situation and beauty of prospect stands unrivalled.' At the time of Griffith's Valuation, the Lynches retained a large estate in the parishes of Rahoon and Moyrus. By June 1869, their estate of 9,565 acres in the parish of Moyrus was advertised for sale;[52] five of eight lots were sold that year. In the early 1870s, the Lynches owned 4,100 acres in the county of Galway plus 1,711 in the county of the city of Galway."

---

[52] See page 23 for a discussion of the 1869 auction of Marcus Lynch's Moyrus estate, including Loughaconeera.

In addition to owning Loughaconeera and seven contiguous townlands, Nicholas Lynch (1804-1862) was the High Sherriff of Galway in 1843. His son Marcus (1836-1916) joined the 33rd (Duke of Wellington's) Regiment in 1855 and resigned his appointment in 1864. Marcus acquired ownership of the property upon his father's death in 1862. In Paris in 1867, Marcus married Blanche, the only daughter of Count Julius Marylski, Duchy of Posen, Leuczyca, Poland. They had two sons who died young and three daughters who became Sisters of Charity at Clarinbridge near Galway. Because there were no children to acquire the property after Marcus' death, his sister Lilly Lynch succeeded to the estate. The property was taken over by the Land Commission in 1923 and sold after Miss Lynch's death in 1930.

An article in the *Freeman's Journal* of 8 November 1916, reported the following upon Marcus' death. "Deep regret will be felt throughout Galway and the West of Ireland at the announcement of the death of Mr. Marcus Lynch, D.L. of Barna House, Galway. …He was an extensive landowner and the direct descendant of one of the thirteen tribes of Galway. He had been Chairman of the Galway Harbor Commissioners for over a quarter of a century, his election on each occasion being unanimous. …He took a deep interest in the little Catholic Church at Barna, of which he was a generous supporter; and he enjoyed the popularity of all classes."

In order to understand the lives of our farmer-fishermen ancestors in Loughaconeera, I sought to learn about Nicholas and Marcus as landlords. Did they "enjoy the popularity of all classes"? Did they support or evict tenants? Why did they put up for sale (in 1869), their estate in Moyrus consisting of Loughaconeera and seven other townlands?

The lineage of the Lynches has been documented extensively but I located only three documents describing their treatment of their tenants. First, the 1869 Moyrus sales notice states that they had not raised rents for 20 years (since before the Great Famine) and they invested 7,000 pounds in improvements to the property (page 23). Second, a notice appeared in the Barna Golf Club Notes in 1905, after Marcus Lynch leased some of his land to the Club. Golf Club Notes mentioned that one of his tenants wrote a ballad, "Linseach Bhearna" praising Marcus Lynch. For the third set of documents about the Lynch's treatment of tenants, I turned to Bridget Anne Hughes, who had translated stories by Sean O'Briain for this family history. I asked Bridget to seek a copy of the ballad, translate it into English, and learn about the history of the ballad.

Bridget Anne located a book with lyrics of Irish songs from that era, *Leabhar Mor na nAmhran*, including the song Línseach Bhearna (Lynch of Barna). A recommendation in that book led Bridget Anne to a second book, *Traditional Songs from Connemara* by Mairtin Pheats O'Cualain. Bridget Anne found this background in the second book:

"The song Linseach Bhearna is about a member of the Lynch family, one of the major tribes and landowners of Galway. He (*note from Joyce – either Nicholas or his son Marcus*) evicted a woman who was unable to pay her rent. She composed a satire about him, which embarrassed and angered him (*note from Joyce – Bridget Anne could not locate a copy of this satire*). She later regretted it and composed the song Línseach Bhearna which praised and flattered him instead. It is reported in folklore that she was subsequently allowed to return to the house from which she had been evicted." Bridget Anne translated the lyrics of Linseach Bhearna (on the following page), and she located this recording at https://seannos.tg4.ie/baile/amhranaithe/caitlin-ni-chualain/linseach-bhearna-amhrain-is-ansa-liom/. We could not locate any additional records to determine and document the extent to which poor treatment by their Lynch landlords may have prompted our Joyce ancestors to emigrate to the United States, as happened with thousands of other Irish tenants. But, surely, the lack of land and opportunities in Ireland were major factors in their emigration decisions.

**Barna House, County Galway, seen from an estuary of Galway Bay**

**Photo from the National University of Galway, Landed Estates Databas**

**During the late 19th century, a tenant wrote this ballad, Línseach Bhearna, praising her Lynch landlord. Translated by Bridget Anne Hughes.**

## Línseach Bhearna

Ag goil ó Chasla aniar is mé lag tuirseach de mo thriall, I mBearna is ea d'iarr mé áras.
Fuaireas sin gan mhoill in aice leis an gcoill, San áit a bhfásann cnó agus airní.

Ó, déanfar droichead óir ar Pholl an Oistre fós,
Is beidh airgead i stórtha an Mháistir,
Arm seasta i gcóir ag tíocht ag déanamh spóirt,
Ag amharc ar an ógfhear álainn.

Fíon is puins go leor a bheas eadrainn ar bord,
Sláinte fear dhá ól trí ráithe.
Siúd séan ar an oidhre óg nach scarfaidh leis go deo,
Is beidh bua Chonnacht ag Línseach Bhearna.

Is tá loingis ag an Línseach a rinneadh ins an tír seo
De choillte is de chrainnte a d'fhás dó.
Is gléasfar cabhlach cruinn i bhfoirm ceart is i gcaoi Is beidh a ngunnaí ar a dtaobh ag lámhach.

Nach mór an spórt sa tír nuair a bheas an chabhlach linn,
Beidh a gcuid slata seoil faoi shíodaí bána,
Anois tá an chabhlach cruinn is tiocfaidh anall an Rí,

Is beidh sé ar chuairt mhíosa i mBearna.

Céard a dhéanfas muid ansiúd má théann sé choíchin anonn?
Titfidh an dúiche uilig faoi smúit mar gheall air,
Is chuaigh na meacha ó dhiúl a gcuid meala le teann cumha,
Is na héanlaithe, scaoil siad a gclúmh le fána.

An Línseach álainn úd a bhfuil na diamonds os a chomhair
A dtig iasc ar chuile chuan mar gheall air,
Is gur deise gnúis a shúil' ná na réalta maidin dhrúcht', Is é is samhail dhó bláth na n-úll sa ngairdín.

Is fásann cruithneacht fhéin san áit a siúlann sé,
Chomh fairsing is atá féar glas i mBearna,
Is gile a thaobh ná an t-aol, is deirge a ghrua ná an chaor,
Nuair a aibíonn sí ar chraobh i ngleannta.

Tá iníon Rí na Gréige ag fáil bháis le cumha ina dhiaidh,
Is níor chodail a súil néal le trí ráithe,
Is go b'éard a dúirt briathra a béil gur aingeal é fhéin,
A bhíodh i gcomhluadar Mhic Dé na nGrásta.

## Lynch of Barna

On my way over from Casla weak and tired of my journey,
In Barna I looked for lodging.
Which I found without delay beside the wood,
Where nuts and sloes grow.

Oh, there will be a gold bridge across The Pool of The Oysters, and silver in the Master's stores,
An army is readied for entertainment Looking at the beautiful young man.

Plenty of wine and punch between us on board, To drink a man's health for 9 months.
May the young heir always be happy and prosperous, And Lynch of Barna will be the greatest man in Connacht.

Lynch has ships that were made in this country Of woods and trees that grew for him.
A well-crafted fleet will be made
And there will be guns shooting from their sides.

What sport in the country when the fleet will be with us,
Their sails will be made of white silk,
When the fleet is complete the King will come over, And he will visit for a month in Barna.

What will we do if Lynch ever leaves?
The whole area will be under a cloud of darkness, And in sorrow the bees will neglect their nature for honey,
And the birds will shed their feathers.

That beautiful Lynch who has diamonds before him That fish come to every harbour for him,
And the look in his eyes is finer than the dew of morning,
And he is the image of apple blossom in the garden.

The wheat itself grows where he walks,
As widespread as green grass in Barna,
His complexion is brighter than whitewash,
his cheek is redder than the berry,
when it ripens on a branch in the valleys.

The king of Greece's daughter is pining for him,
And her eyes have not slept a wink in 9 months,
And her words say that he is an angel,
Who was with the merciful Son of God.

# Appendix Nine

## Highlights of Galway City's Early History[53]

"Galway is the fifth largest city in Ireland and the only city in the province of Connaught. It takes its name from the River Corrib or *Abhainn na Gaillimhe* and was established in 1124 by the King of Connaught, Turlough Mór O'Connor when he constructed a fort at the mouth of the river. The Ó Flaithbheartaighs or O'Flahertys held the city until Richard Mor de Burgh led the Normans, who had already conquered much of Ireland in the 12th century, to finally seize the city in the 1230s. Over time, the de Burgh or Burke dynasty of Clanrickard fought among themselves while simultaneously integrating with the Gaelic Irish.

17<sup>th</sup> century map of Galway City

Contemporary Galway City

"In 1333, the city of Galway, led by fourteen merchant families who gave the city its nickname as 'The City of The Tribes,' sought independence from the volatile Clanrickard Burkes. The town was surrounded by a defensive wall and in 1396, finally secured its charter from the English Crown. For centuries, the Tribes of Galway dominated the economic, political, and social life of Galway City, distinguishing themselves from the Norman and Gaelic residents of rural areas.

"The fourteen Catholic merchant families who controlled Galway from the mid-13<sup>th</sup> to the late 19<sup>th</sup> centuries were Athy, Blake, Bodkin, Browne, D'Arcy, Deane, Font, French, **Joyce**, Kirwan, Lynch, Martyn, Morris and Skerrett. They descended from the Gaels, Normans, Flemish, French, and English. Twelve were Anglo-Normans[54] while D'Arcy and Kirwan were Normandised Irish Gaels (natives of Ireland). They took the Confederate side in the English Civil War, were punished by Cromwell, and lost their political power to the Parliamentarians who had their property confiscated.

---

[53] This text is from the "definitive" publication per Irish historians, *The History of the Town and County of the Town of Galway,* by James Hardiman, W. Folds and Sons, Dublin, 1828. See http://www.askaboutireland.ie/reading-room/

[54] Normans were Vikings who settled in NW France in the 10<sup>th</sup> and 11<sup>th</sup> centuries and their descendants. The Normans conquered England in 1066. Anglo-Normans refer to Normans living in England after 1066.

"The restoration of the Stuart monarchy in 1660 improved the fortunes of the 'tribesmen'. However, after the Catholic defeat at the Battle of the Boyne in 1690 and a siege of the city, political power passed to a Protestant minority who remained dominant until the 19th century. Persecution of the Catholic merchant families caused Galway to become an economic backwater.

"The O'Flaherty Gaelic clan led Gaelic resistance to English rule for centuries with their stronghold in Connemara to the east of Lough Corrib–the dividing line between their territory and that of the Clanrickard Burkes. Following the Cromwellian invasion of Ireland, the leading Gaelic and Old English Catholic landowners were infamously banished 'to hell or to Connaught' and took refuge in Galway. With poor agricultural farmland and a lack of modernization, County Galway was disadvantaged compared to the rest of Ireland." (End of quotation from *The History of the Town and County of Galway*, by James Hardiman, 1828).

**They Stayed on the Farm**

Irish widow with her only child
who did not emigrate.
1935 Dorothy Lange Collection,
Oakland Museum.

Irish widow carrying turf in a creel.
Date unknown

Made in the USA
Monee, IL
07 October 2024

67361858R00055